"This book will be a game-changer - not only does it provide essential information for assessing and supporting children with dyslexia, but also strategies to empower teachers to utilise these tools and their own skills to help all children! The book replaces confusion with clarity, and this alone will be welcomed by teachers. Despite many initiatives in dyslexia, there are still too many uncertainties shared by many. Louise Selby provides a superb chronicle of the developments in dyslexia and brings us all up-to-date and dispels many myths in the process. This is a very clear guide for teachers illustrating what the research looks like in practice, including a very useful appendix on interpreting a diagnostic assessment report and a range of intervention approaches to suit all budgets with many of the tools costing very little. The book encompasses a whole-learning approach, including strategies on learning skills to equip the learner to be self-sufficient and independent - beyond school. Without doubt an empowering and essential book!"

Dr Gavin Reid, *Author and Psychologist, Co-director The Reading Lab. Inc., Vancouver*

"*All About Dyslexia* is a practical and clear-sighted book, with the authentic voices of adults and young people with experience of dyslexia woven through every page. Louise clearly explains the challenges presented by dyslexia and dispels some of the commonly held myths that lead to confusion about how best to teach these learners. Her emphasis on quick wins, practical, low-cost classroom-based strategies and individual strengths will help teachers across the age ranges and subjects support all their students not just to survive, but to thrive."

Bridget Thornhill, *Senior Teacher for Dyslexia, Nottinghamshire County Council*

"In her opening chapter, Louise describes her personal interest in dyslexia as 'fascinating and hopeful' and this book is exactly that. The child voice included throughout is powerful and Louise has been generous in sharing a wealth of practical ideas which makes this essential reading for all teaching staff. The layout is easy to dip into, with top tips for success, quick wins and photographs - perfect for bite-sized CPD. This is a hopeful book that not only shows the impact teachers can have with a few adaptations and really good teaching - but also provides them with the tools to do it."

Felicity Nichols, *SEND Adviser, HFL Education*

"This book is a must-have for every classroom and home where young people have barriers to learning. Louise's style of presenting information with clarity, practical examples and ideas for further support is invaluable. I read this in one sitting, scribbling notes to use, from both a parent and professional perspective. Louise provides theory and background to help understand the evolution of our current view of dyslexia and how this has shaped the support provided and the perspectives of those involved. There is a wealth of information to take away and use immediately. I highly recommend this book to all."

Dr Sarah Moseley, *Educational Consultant, Inclusion, SEND, and Literacy Specialist*

"Dyslexia has been a word within the teaching profession that we have all known for so long but has always caused much confusion. For many, including myself, my knowledge has come from books, articles online, and the knowledge of children I have taught but this has led to a jumble of thinking! But this is about to change! *All About Dyslexia* is a book that every class teacher and leader should read. It's clear, knowledgeable and practical! Louise clearly sets out what dyslexia is and the impact on a child, but most importantly the practical and manageable techniques teachers can use to help children learn! So many of the strategies will help all pupils in the class. A must-read!"

Mags Sexton, *Head Teacher Westcourt Primary School, Kent*

"This book is a must for anyone who works with children and young people in schools; packed full of realistic and practical ideas, with a balance of theory and practice, and relevant to today's education systems. I can't wait to share it with our schools!"

Alison Szalay, *Senior Specialist Advisory Teacher for SEND (Cognition and Learning)*

"Louise Selby's book is a game-changer for primary educators, SENCOs and parents seeking to support dyslexic learners. This comprehensive guide offers innovative strategies and fresh insights that transform teaching approaches and learning environments. It empowers teachers to create inclusive, supportive settings where every child can thrive. Unique to this guide are practical, classroom-ready techniques like tactile letters and visual mnemonics for spelling, engaging phonics games, and effective reading interventions. Additionally, it fosters strong collaboration with parents, creating a supportive network for each child and providing effective approaches that make a real difference."

Abigail Hawkins, *(FCCT), SEN Consultant, SENsible SENCO*

"*All About Dyslexia* is a well-planned and sequenced guide for educators, offering clear and practical strategies to support dyslexic students across the primary curriculum. It provides insight into the experiences of dyslexic learners, highlighting their challenges and successes. The book is well-organised, covering each subject area with evidence-based approaches that are easy to implement, such as phonics-based reading techniques and concrete methods for teaching mathematics. Emphasising an inclusive classroom environment, the author advocates for recognising the strengths of dyslexic students and adapting teaching methods to meet their needs. This book is a must-read for educators dedicated to fostering a supportive and inclusive learning atmosphere."

Adriana Verrecchia, *Primary Specialist SEN Consultant for a multi-academy trust.*

"Dyslexic children, their teachers and parents will thank Louise for producing such a comprehensive and accessible guide to this area. Practical and highly relevant strategies are suggested which are achievable and relevant to day-to-day classroom practice, with potentially complex areas presented in a highly accessible and supportive way. Louise has achieved great things with this book. Highly recommended!"

Sally-Ann Morrison, *Founder and Director of Praxis CPD*

"Reading, writing and spelling support can be highly variable across settings, with over-reliance on a small set of strategies and interventions that don't work for all dyslexic children. It's common as a Speech and Language Therapist to see entrenched and entwined language and reading challenges, with children feeling bad about learning. I loved the flexible advice in this book, which gives quick wins as well as more involved strategies that encourage individualised support with an emphasis on independence. There is a lot to inform and extend the work of Speech and Language Therapists as well as educators in this book."

Angharad Welch, *Speech and Language Therapist, Find the Key Speech and Language Therapy*

"Within the time constraints of teachers' workload, this book is an easy read with clarity, up-to-date research and set out with lots of practical ideas and advice. As I read through the strategies, I realised how they could be utilised for whole-staff training of quality-first teaching. It's the sort of book you can put down and pick up as needed. I especially liked the simple format of the 'Quick Wins', something that we all look for in today's teaching climate. The voice of the child is so important as it gives true life insight into the difficulties that our young people face, and their need to be part of the process of support in order to be engaged. The book covers everything from early reading through to written techniques for KS2 children. I'm excited to see the book published!"

Clare Lewis, *Head of School, Lime Tree Primary Academy*

"This book is packed full of ideas and tips for how to plan learning in a way that is inclusive and supportive of dyslexic learners, so that they can experience success and be enabled to work to their potential, but it is also, as the author says, about learning how to teach everyone 'really, really well'. The voices of those with dyslexia giving their perspective on education makes a powerful case for the use of these ideas in our classrooms. The author has a very readable style and helps the reader understand why it is important to plan and teach in this way by underpinning it all with just enough of the theory without it becoming dry or heavy to read. It is a book that can be dipped into for ideas again and again. It should be a compulsory read for all teachers and student teachers; I wish it had been around when I was a class teacher!"

Anne Langley, *School-based Specialist Teacher*

"I highly recommend this book; academic research is skilfully interlaced with practical ideas for supporting dyslexic pupils in the classroom. The design of the book allows teachers, both new to the profession and more experienced colleagues, to read the book cover to cover or to select specific topics. Louise Selby writes in an easily accessible style and respects her readers; the 'Quick Wins' and 'Top Tips' mean that even the busiest teacher will find something they can introduce to their lessons to support dyslexic learners without too much effort."

Anna Fenelon, *Buckinghamshire Specialist Teacher for Cognition and Learning*

"*All About Dyslexia* is current and relevant, including the updated definition of dyslexia and latest research that informs practice. Louise explores learning differences that are so often part of dyslexia, including metacognition and self-regulated learning as well as reading, writing and spelling. This is an informative, accessible and engaging read, suitable for all educators and parents, and Louise's empathy shines through. Throughout the book, practical solutions and strategies appropriate to support children at all stages in primary are given. The examples from dyslexic learners and real school case studies bring to life some of the realities these learners experience at school and the strategies used to support them in their learning."

Hazel McPake, *M. Ed (SEN), Tutor specialising in supporting and teaching pupils with dyslexia and other literacy difficulties*

"*All About Dyslexia* by Louise Selby is an essential resource for anyone working with students with dyslexia. This book stands out for its clear, concise and easy-to-read format, making it an indispensable tool for both new and experienced educators. It is packed with practical tips and strategies, with each chapter ending with 'Quick Wins', empowering teachers to create engaging and effective learning environments for their dyslexic learners."

Hema Desai, *Speech and Language Therapist/ Specialist Teacher, Director of Connect: Literacy, Speech and Language Services*

"In her new book, Louise delivers an honest, respectful and invaluably practical insight into the world of dyslexia. The content is chunked, detailed and includes real-life stories to give the reader a deeper understanding of what it 'feels' like to be a dyslexic. Louise has thought of everything and caters to everyone's needs, demonstrating simple, cost-effective methods of support for the teacher in the classroom, the tutor and the parent/carer at home. Based on the latest scientific research, Louise assures practical guidance and direction for those of us who support students with dyslexia and presents a well-meaning book with advice that practitioners will be speaking about and sharing for years to come."

Sharon Hall, *MA, Dip (SEN), Founder Dyslexia Routes, Dyslexia Tutor and Trainer*

Access your Online Resources

All About Dyslexia is accompanied by a number of printable online materials, designed to ensure this resource best supports your professional needs.

Go to https://resourcecentre.routledge.com/speechmark and click on the cover of this book.

Answer the question prompt using your copy of the book to gain access to the online content.

ALL ABOUT DYSLEXIA

All About Dyslexia is an accessible and informative guide for primary school teachers, designed to increase their understanding of dyslexia and enhance their toolkit with practical, adaptable strategies to support learners with dyslexia and specific learning difficulties in their setting.

The book debunks myths and misconceptions and clearly defines dyslexia, shining a light on a different way of thinking and learning. It then looks at metacognition and dyslexia across the curriculum, with a focus on grounding literacy skills and supporting the foundations of reading. Drawing on the experience of the learners themselves, the book equips teachers with strategies for high-quality teaching that will benefit all learners, not just those with dyslexia. *All About Dyslexia* includes:

- Chapters that are easy to dip in and out of, with top tips and signposting to further resources and research.
- A wealth of up-to-date, evidence-based, practical strategies for everyday practice at the coalface, including 'quick wins' which provide easy, prep-free ideas for planning that can be implemented straight away.
- The voices of learners with dyslexia, parents and practitioners woven throughout, offering an important insight into 'how I do things differently'.
- An overview of different interventions, assistive technology and dyslexia-friendly environments with printable resources for use in the classroom.
- Ways to collaborate effectively with parents and carers to best support dyslexic learners' progress.

This easy-to-read book focuses on difference rather than deficit and is a valuable resource to empower primary educators, demystifying dyslexia and providing the strategies needed to feel confident meeting learners' needs. It will be essential reading for all primary school educators, SENCOs and parents who are supporting children with specific learning difficulties.

Louise Selby is a dyslexia specialist trainer, consultant, author, assessor and teacher. She has 25 years' experience of working with SEND within Hertfordshire local authority in teaching, SENCO and advisory roles. She now works freelance, providing training and consultancy for schools as well as dyslexia assessment. Louise believes in partnership and collaboration and this is at the heart of all that she does. She is also the author of *Morph Mastery: Morphological Intervention for Reading, Spelling and Vocabulary*.

ALL ABOUT SEND

Series Advisor: Natalie Packer

All About SEND provides busy teachers and SENCOs with essential guidance and practical strategies to effectively support learners with special educational needs and disabilities. Each accessible and informative book focuses on a common area of need and explores key traits and terminology, debunks myths and misconceptions, and introduces readers to a range of easy-to-implement ideas for practice and concrete solutions to everyday challenges.

ALL ABOUT AUTISM
A Practical Guide to Supporting Autistic Learners in the Primary School
Lynn McCann

ALL ABOUT AUTISM
A Practical Guide to Supporting Autistic Learners in the Secondary School
Lynn McCann

ALL ABOUT DYSCALCULIA
A Practical Guide to Supporting Learners with Dyscalculia in the Primary School
Judy Hornigold

ALL ABOUT SEMH
A Practical Guide to Supporting Learners with Social, Emotional and Mental Health Needs in the Primary School
Sarah Johnson

ALL ABOUT SEMH
A Practical Guide to Supporting Learners with Social, Emotional and Mental Health Needs in the Secondary School
Sarah Johnson

ALL ABOUT DYSLEXIA

A PRACTICAL GUIDE FOR PRIMARY TEACHERS

Louise Selby

Routledge
Taylor & Francis Group
LONDON AND NEW YORK

Designed cover image: Getty Images

First published 2025
by Routledge
4 Park Square, Milton Park, Abingdon, Oxon OX14 4RN

and by Routledge
605 Third Avenue, New York, NY 10158

Routledge is an imprint of the Taylor & Francis Group, an informa business

British Library Cataloguing-in-Publication Data
A catalogue record for this book is available from the British Library

ISBN: 978-1-032-51291-4 (hbk)
ISBN: 978-1-032-51287-7 (pbk)
ISBN: 978-1-003-40154-4 (ebk)

DOI: 10.4324/9781003401544

Typeset in Interstate
by Deanta Global Publishing Services, Chennai, India

Access the Support Material:
https://resourcecentre.routledge.com/speechmark

MIX
Paper | Supporting responsible forestry
FSC® C013056

Printed and bound in Great Britain by
TJ Books Limited, Padstow, Cornwall

I dedicate this book to my mum, Rosemary, whose writing talent inspired us all, and her sister Sandra, my most avid supporter. Their relentless commitment to learning will never be forgotten.

CONTENTS

FOREWORD

All teachers are teachers of learners with special educational needs and disabilities (SEND). Those professionals who work in truly inclusive schools will understand that SEND is everyone's responsibility. However, the situation has not always been like this. When I started my teaching career over thirty years ago, learners who had additional needs were more likely to be seen as the responsibility of the special educational needs coordinator (SENCO). As the person in school who 'held' the SEND knowledge and expertise, the SENCO would often be a lone force in championing, and meeting, the needs of this particular group of learners.

The picture in education is somewhat different today. The profile of the children and young people we teach continues to change; the impact of the COVID pandemic, for example, has led to an increase in those identified with gaps in their learning or with mental health concerns. The number of learners with complex needs being educated within mainstream schools also continues to rise. As professionals, we now have a greater awareness and understanding of some of the challenges our learners face and, as a result, are more determined to do our best to support them to achieve. We understand that this cannot be the role of one person – the SENCO – alone. Every teacher needs to be a teacher of SEND.

Teaching learners with SEND may be one of the most rewarding things you ever do in your classroom. When you observe a learner who has really struggled to grasp a new idea or concept finally achieve their 'lightbulb moment', it's all the sweeter knowing the amount of effort they have put in to get there. However, teaching learners with SEND can also be one of the most challenging aspects of your career. In a 2019 survey[1] carried out by the Department for Education (DfE) in England, the level of confidence amongst teachers in supporting learners with SEND was reported as very low. Relevant professional development in this area is, at best, patchy; only 41 per cent of the teachers surveyed by the DfE felt there was sufficient SEND training in place for all teachers. Several years on from this study and the picture is similar; as the complexity of SEND in mainstream classrooms grows, teachers are feeling the pressure to develop further knowledge and skills to meet need effectively.

So how do we overcome this challenge? Evidence suggests that the best place to start is through the delivery of inclusive, high-quality teaching (HQT). As the Education Endowment Foundation (EEF) report[2] tells us, there is no 'magic bullet' for teaching learners with SEND and, to a great extent, good teaching for those with SEND is good teaching for all. This means we need to develop a repertoire of effective teaching strategies such as scaffolding, explicit instruction and use of technology, then use these strategies flexibly to meet the needs of individuals or groups of learners.

Although a focus on effective HQT in the classroom is the starting point, some learners will require more specific teaching methods to meet their individual needs. There is no substitute for really getting to know a child or young person so you can fully understand their personal strengths, potential barriers to learning and what works for them in the classroom. However, it can still be helpful for us as professionals to develop a more general understanding of some of the common areas of need we are likely to come across and to have a range of strategies we can try implementing within our practice. This is where *All About SEND* can help.

The *All About SEND* series of books aim to support every teacher to be a teacher of SEND. Each book has been designed to enable teachers, and other professionals such as support staff, to develop their knowledge and understanding of how to effectively promote teaching and learning for those with identified areas of need. The books provide essential information and a range of practical strategies for supporting learners in the classroom. Written by expert practitioners, the guidance has been informed by a wealth of first-hand experience, with the views of children and young people with SEND and their parents taking centre stage.

This book, *All About Dyslexia: A Practical Guide for Primary Teachers*, focuses on supporting learners who struggle with literacy, specifically those with processing difficulties that affect the acquisition of reading and spelling. As a dyslexia specialist teacher and assessor with significant educational experience, the author Louise Selby shares her infectious passion for supporting schools to empower learners to reach their full potential. *All About Dyslexia: A Practical Guide for Primary Teachers* provides a wealth of information on the up-to-date research around dyslexia and helps to debunk some of the common myths using robust evidence and the voice of the learner. Importantly, the book contains a wide range of easy-to-use, everyday practical strategies that teachers can apply in the classroom, demonstrating that teaching learners with dyslexia is synonymous with teaching all learners effectively.

Thank you for choosing to read this book and for embracing the challenge of responsibility: every teacher is a teacher of SEND.

Natalie Packer,
SEND Consultant, Director of NPEC Ltd.
@NataliePacker

NOTES

1 HM Government (2022). *SEND Review: Right support, right place, right time. Government consultation on the SEND and alternative provision system in England.* https://assets.publishing.service.gov.uk/government/uploads/system/uploads/attachment_data/file/1063620/SEND_review_right_support_right_place_right_time_accessible.pdf (p. 42).
2 Education Endowment Foundation (2020). Special Education Needs in Mainstream Schools. https://educationendowmentfoundation.org.uk/education-evidence/guidance-reports/send

ACKNOWLEDGEMENTS

All About Dyslexia has been a team effort, as every educational project should be. I hope it does justice to the numerous contributors, whose generous sharing of experiences, advice, recommendations and stories have made the book the shared story that it is. I have learned so much through writing it, as I hope you will from reading.

I am indebted to all the "Voices of Dyslexia" participants, both those who have shared through film (Brock, Lorna, Alex, Sara, Lisa, Gill, Pippa, Rachel, Lindsay, Sara, Harry, Oliver, Louise, Fred, Jamie, Molly, Aaro) and those who preferred to remain anonymous. Thank you to the schools and teachers who have supported and advised, especially Sarah Pearce at Zouch Academy and Mollie Keiley at St Joseph and St Bede Primary, and to all those who engaged with my social media posts as I gathered thoughts and ideas chapter by chapter. Thanks to the wonderful Clare Ashworth and Molly Kavanagh at Speechmark, as well as Natalie Packer, for their patience, advice and constructive proofreading. Anne, Alison, Claire, Clare, Katharine, Mags and Sally-Ann for proofreading and feedback. My husband and son for coping so admirably with my "writing days".

HEARING FROM THE EXPERTS

Authorship of this book has really been a team effort, and I am indebted to so many people for sharing their experiences with me to help me shape this book. This includes children and adults who have dyslexia, parents, teachers, educational psychologists and schools.

VOICES OF DYSLEXIA

The book is interspersed with quotes from individuals. These quotes were taken from a number of sources. A number of them were provided on film, which can be viewed on the Voices of Dyslexia project page[1] on my website. This be accessed via the QR code.

Other participants preferred to share their story in writing or by interview, and to remain anonymous. These individuals have been quoted, but all names have been changed.

CASE STUDIES

I am deeply grateful to schools who offered to share their good practice in the form of images and case studies. Images of this good practice can be found in Chapter 11 (are also available in colour on my website, accessible via the QR code), and case studies are below.

Louise Selby Dyslexia

ZOUCH ACADEMY AND NURSERY, TIDWORTH (https://zouch-academy.twhf.org.uk)

"It's just common practice. These are easy things to do."

Sarah Pearce, SENCO

Zouch Academy, in Tidworth, Wiltshire, is close to a military base. It embarked on its journey towards Dyslexia Friendly accreditation by the British Dyslexia Association in 2020, and achieved the accreditation mark in 2022. According to Sarah, big changes were not necessary: it was more about enhancing strategies they had in place for individual children so that all benefited – for example, setting the whiteboard background to a pastel colour as a response to one child using yellow paper.

"You still have individual needs, but the majority of what we did was at a whole class level."

Sarah Pearce

Assistive technology has been transformative. Talking tins (voice recorders) and talking whiteboards are in regular use, and an investment in Clicker software proved very beneficial for children with writing difficulties. Some children use laptops, because their typing speed is better and they benefit from having a word bank, spellcheck and setting the laptop screen to a pastel colour. Reading pens have been trialled and are now used as part of normal practice, and improvement in reading has been observed as a result. Widgit symbols are used consistently for vocabulary on display, which has helped all children. Alphabets and physical resources are available for children to get independently.

The impact has been seen not just in learner attainment but also in behaviour. Children who displayed negative behaviour previously are more able to access the curriculum, resulting in more positive engagement. Training staff has been essential, especially with new assistive technology.

In terms of embedding practice, what has helped the most is teachers seeing the impact for themselves. The challenge has been in how to engage parents. Sarah has found that inviting them in regularly, and breaking down what the school was doing into steps has helped remove these barriers. Showing parents that the strategies used for dyslexia are used for all children has been transformative in reducing the stigma of learning difficulties and improving parental engagement.

ST. JOSEPH AND ST. BEDE RC PRIMARY SCHOOL, BURY (www.sjsb.stoccat.org.uk)

Voices of Dyslexia

"It's second nature to us."

Mollie Keiley, SENCO

St Joseph and St Bede, which is in a deprived area of Bury, began its journey towards Dyslexia Friendly status in 2014, when the headteacher, Jane Myerscough, noticed a number of needs in Year 4. By the time this cohort left the school, accreditation from Action Dyslexia had been gained, with support from Bury Local Authority. It has been an ongoing journey of reviewing and adapting as new staff and children come in.

The school uses an online learning platform (Seesaw) which, according to Mollie, is their "biggest win". Children who struggle to get their ideas on to paper can record their voices and upload images or even films on to Seesaw, and many alternative methods of recording are in use, which benefit all children. Children use assistive technology features on iPads as a matter of course.

Resource stations are available in each class. These include accessible dictionaries, recordable whiteboards, reading rulers, cream-coloured paper, word mats, tactile letters, number lines and strings, counters, different types of pens and pencil grips and multi-sensory spelling resources. Independence is key for all learners; they know what is available, how to find it, how to use it and how it could help. All children, whatever their ability, are encouraged to use physical resources.

Mental health is prioritised, and each class has a calm-down pod. The pastoral worker understands the frustration that dyslexia can cause. Displays are colour-coded, with images to support words, and different types of recording are on display. All resources are clearly labelled with images as well as words. Every year there is a "no pens Wednesday" which is thoroughly enjoyed by everyone.

Training staff has been central. Teachers have been trained in how to use teaching assistants effectively. All teaching assistants receive training in dyslexia. All new staff also receive training, and there is a checklist of "non-negotiables" for the learning environment. Each teacher is placed in a cross-phase triad to observe and support each other, and each term the school has a focus for this. Every Friday, the teaching assistants are allocated time with the teacher during assembly.

Transition is a strong focus, and learners have provision maps and pupil passports which are shared with teachers and parents. Good relationships with parents are a high priority, and there is an open-door policy for parents. Parents are encouraged to contribute to pupil passports. Family literacy is a whole-school priority, but this is a work in progress, and some parents are difficult to engage.

Ironically, the challenge for St Joseph and St Bede's has been early identification. Because of the strategies that are so well embedded, sometimes children who are found later to have dyslexia cope well at St Joseph's and St Bede's. They are working on this transition.

NOTE

1 Selby, L. (2024) Voices of Dyslexia. https://louiseselby-dyslexia.com/voices-of-dyslexia-do-you-have-a-story-to-tell

Part 1

INTRODUCING DYSLEXIA

1

DYSLEXIA: CONTEXT, MYTHS AND DEFINITIONS

My journey with dyslexia began when I learned what it meant to fail. I was one of the lucky ones who sailed through school, university and teacher training. Although gruelling, my early years of teaching were exciting and zany. Dancing on tables to *The Muppets* during all-day Technology lessons with Year 4 is a favourite memory (these were the days before health and safety!). After some years of teaching, however, I was struck by a debilitating illness, and for the first time in my life, I learned what it was like to really struggle with what should have been easy. After years of brain fog and mobility problems, I dragged myself out the other side of what had been diagnosed as chronic fatigue syndrome (CFS). The onset of CFS sparked my interest (and empathy) in special educational needs and disabilities (SEND). If I had not learned what it meant to struggle, I do not believe I would have been driven to support others in equivalent situations in education.

Why dyslexia? For me, dyslexia is both fascinating and hopeful. Given the right adjustments and support, there is so much potential for learners with dyslexia to succeed. I fully believe that learning to teach children and young people with dyslexia is synonymous with learning how to teach your class really, really well. There is undoubtedly a place for targeted intervention, but meeting the needs of learners with dyslexia starts in the classroom. It is a great frustration of mine that over my career I have met many great class teachers who already had many

DOI: 10.4324/9781003401544-2

of the tools they needed to meet the needs of learners with dyslexia, and yet they felt ill-equipped because dyslexia was to them somehow mysterious. I want this to change!

This is my drive and the purpose of this book. It is primarily for teachers at the coalface. If you can teach well, you can teach learners with dyslexia well. My intention is threefold. First, I hope to enable teachers to understand and feel confident that they can meet needs in the class by being great teachers. Second, I hope to equip them in this by providing strategies across the curriculum. Finally my hope is to empower them to change the narrative, so that adjustments are available for all learners to thrive, whether diagnosed with dyslexia or not.

In this introductory chapter, we'll take a quick dive into the history of dyslexia in order to understand the backdrop and dispel some myths. The definition of dyslexia will follow, with explanation of what it looks like in the classroom. We'll finish with a look at how dyslexia is diagnosed.

A LOOK AT LANGUAGE

There is no consensus on how we should refer to dyslexia. Some prefer the "person first" approach – that is, "person with dyslexia" and "having dyslexia". Others prefer the label to be central because it is a strong part of their identity, bringing strengths as well as challenges, therefore preferring "dyslexic person". The language used in this book will alternate between both variations, acknowledging that the experience of the child is paramount.

LEARNING FROM HISTORY

> In a little under a century and a half, dyslexia has gone from a poorly understood problem, the scope and scale of which was unknown, to one of the most widely recognised learning difficulties in the world.[1]

As I write, today (10 May 2024) marks the end of a momentous week in British history. This week, a new definition of dyslexia was published. For the first time in dyslexia's almost 150 years of history, multiple stakeholders have come together to find consensus on a new definition of a condition which has caused controversy for as many years.

Why has dyslexia been so controversial, and does it matter? To move forward, we must focus on common ground, not controversy. However, to help us do this fully, and to once and for all dispel some unhelpful myths about dyslexia, it is useful to understand a little about dyslexia's history, so this is where I will begin.

The first child thought to have what we now call dyslexia was identified in 1896.[2] This was Percy, aged 14, whose inability to learn to read, in spite of his intelligence and persistent teaching, was surprising. Percy was described as suffering from 'congenital word blindness', and this concept is in fact still occasionally (but incorrectly) used by laypeople today.

MYTH: DYSLEXIA IS A VISUAL PROBLEM

Not true! Dyslexia is popularly thought to cause visual problems like moving letters, but this is not the case. "Research indicates that difficulties with visual stress are separable from dyslexia and should be treated separately."[3] While word blindness was used historically as a term to describe dyslexia, we now know that dyslexia is not a visual difficulty.

In the early 1900s in the United States, a clinic for dyslexic learners was established by Samuel Orton, adopting teaching methods which are still used today.[4] During this time of advancement in the US, however, scepticism was a theme in Britain (which we will see would continue to the present day). Cyril Burt, the first educational psychologist to be appointed to a British government body, decided that the concept of dyslexia, or word blindness, was "something of a ruse" and "a product of poor teaching and unfocused students",[5] which, rather than being a persistent developmental condition, could be cured by decent teaching. Burt's argument was appealing to policy makers, who were, of course, also budget controllers.

This scepticism continued and took root, even into very recent years, with an ongoing debate about the purpose of and evidence for dyslexia diagnosis.[6] What is interesting about Burt is his criticism of the role of "non-specialist" parents, especially mothers, in the advancement of dyslexia. He argued that they were unqualified and prejudiced, and should be ignored. But the influence and pivotal role of mothers was to continue, and was, in fact, a key factor in the advancement of provision for dyslexia.

In 1963, the Word Blind Centre was established in London, which formalised dyslexia's footing in UK education. Unfortunately, an unforeseen outcome was that dyslexia became termed "a middle-class syndrome", due to the demographic profile of the children assisted by the Centre. Policymakers had again been served a concept (this time middle-class privilege) that enabled them to reject the existence of dyslexia, and this unhelpful concept lives on today.

MYTH: DYSLEXIA IS MIDDLE-CLASS, FOR THOSE WHO CAN PAY FOR IT

This should not be true! The pattern of education's history has meant that middle classes have been instrumental in the early recognition of dyslexia. Sadly, it is still true in many parts of the UK that dyslexia diagnosis is only available to paying parents, and that those who can pay are those who get supported.

Voices of Dyslexia

"To have a diagnosis, a piece of paper to say help this child be the best they can be, don't ignore what she could achieve with just a little support, to say don't forget her, she counts, is for me, invaluable

> *- but also blooming expensive so has not been gained yet."*
>
> Hazel, parent

My personal passion is to work towards equity, and I'm encouraged by the trajectory of events following the establishment of the Word Blind Centre.

Through the 1970s, scepticism continued, to such an extent that Margaret Thatcher's Department for Education and Science refused to recognise dyslexia in 1973 (even though Thatcher herself was known initially to express a desire to support children with dyslexia). Even in 1978, when Mary Warnock was asked to chair an independent review of children's special educational needs, she was forbidden from using the term "dyslexia". In spite of this, various influential dyslexia associations were established at this time, with championing from many invested parents, and the growing evidence base meant that dyslexia was becoming too difficult to ignore. In 1987, dyslexia was formally recognised by the British parliament, and by the 1990s, dyslexia support had become more widely available.

In 1997, the new Blair government placed a strong emphasis (and funding) on education, especially literacy. In the same year, the landmark Phelps High Court case was heard. This case exemplifies how far dyslexia had come, but how contentious it still was. Pamela Phelps had been diagnosed with dyslexia after she left state education in 1990, not in school, in spite of persistent literacy difficulties and a number of psychologist assessments while there. She claimed that by not diagnosing her, Hillingdon Council was responsible for her inadequate literacy skills and reduced employment opportunities. The High Court found in Phelps's favour,[7] which was an enormous win for the cause of dyslexia.

In 2009, the UK government's Rose Review[8] was published. What was pivotal was the fact that Sir Jim Rose identified the high occurrence of dyslexia in disadvantaged socio-economic groups, highlighting the need for equity. The recommendation was made for all children, whatever their socio-economic background and intellectual ability, to have access to specialist teaching. In spite of an ensuing surge of teachers achieving specialist qualifications over the next five years, this has still not been achieved, and budgets have since been drastically cut.

Voices of Dyslexia

> *"Our main struggle has been getting her dyslexia officially recognised. Some LEAs don't diagnose dyslexia; some don't understand it. Unfortunately this can prevent effective support being put into place. I feel like I'm chasing the impossible."*
>
> Evelyn, parent

The inconsistency described by Evelyn is nothing short of inequity, and it grieves me deeply, but I'm hopeful about the new era.

DEFINING DYSLEXIA

In 2021, the Specific Learning Difficulties Standards Committee (SASC) initiated a review of the assessment and definition of dyslexia, culminating in a Delphi study,[9] which finished in April 2024.[10] The process involved professionals across the debate, and a consensus on a definition of dyslexia has been reached. The breadth of this consensus is the most significant in dyslexia's history. This definition is as follows:

> **Nature**
> The nature and developmental trajectory of dyslexia depends on multiple genetic and environmental influences.
>
> **Manifestation**
> Dyslexia is a set of processing difficulties that affect the acquisition of reading and spelling. The most commonly observed cognitive impairment in dyslexia is a difficulty in phonological processing (i.e. in phonological awareness, phonological processing speed or phonological memory). However, phonological difficulties do not fully explain the variability that is observed. Working memory, processing speed and orthographic skills can contribute to the impact of dyslexia.

Impact
In dyslexia, some or all aspects of literacy attainment are weak in relation to age, standard teaching and instruction, and level of other attainments. Across languages and age groups, difficulties in reading and spelling fluency are a key marker of dyslexia.

Variance and co-occurrence
Dyslexic difficulties exist on a continuum and can be experienced to various degrees of severity. Dyslexia can affect the acquisition of other skills, such as mathematics, reading comprehension or learning another language. Dyslexia frequently co-occurs with one or more other developmental difficulties, including developmental language disorder, dyscalculia, ADHD, and developmental coordination disorder.

What does this definition tell us? First, a core defining feature of dyslexia is the impact on reading and spelling. We are also concerned with the underlying processing skills. These can be defined as follows:

- Phonological awareness, the "ability to accurately identify, discriminate between and manipulate the separate units of sounds in words, known as phonemes".[11]
- Phonological processing speed, the "ability to perform relatively simple repetitive cognitive tasks, quickly, accurately and fluently".[12]
- Phonological memory, the "ability to identify accurately, retain briefly, and repeat sequences of sound".[13]
- Working memory, "the ability to maintain and manipulate information in active attention". This is about holding information in mind while working on it.
- Orthographic processing, the ability to form and retrieve letters, letter sequences and spelling patterns.[14] This is about identifying and remembering the written form of letters and spelling patterns.

While dyslexia always impacts reading and/or spelling in some way, the impact can sometimes be seen in fluency rather than accuracy. This is important for older children, who may have learned to read but lack fluency (they are sometimes described as well compensated). A dyslexic learner's literacy difficulties can be unexpected. This may be in relation to other abilities or the level of teaching/intervention they have had. Dyslexia is a continuum, and needs will vary. The trajectory of dyslexia's impact on a school-aged child with dyslexia can be heavily influenced by what is done, or not done, in school (among other factors).

The definition draws our attention to some aspects of dyslexia that are sometimes missed. For some, the most noticeable impact of dyslexia can be on maths, for example. Dyslexia commonly co-occurs with other difficulties, and the learning profile can be complex. As a result, dyslexia is again sometimes unidentified.

WHAT DOES DYSLEXIA LOOK LIKE IN SCHOOL?

In essence, dyslexia is a literacy difficulty. Any child with literacy difficulties *may* therefore have dyslexia. But not all will; there are other explanations for difficulties. Some indicators to look for in primary school are below:

1. Specific reading and/or spelling difficulties in spite of good teaching; slow to acquire phonics skills.
2. Persistent difficulties over time, not sudden onset.
3. Developmental history of some difficulties before literacy was taught, such as speech and language, attention.
4. Familial incidence of dyslexia/literacy difficulties.
5. Literacy difficulties are unexpected in relation to other abilities. For example, the child who is articulate but writing does not match speech, the child who is great with numbers or science, or the child who loves being read to but avoids reading. The child who is creative but cannot write stories. This is not an exhaustive list: unexpectedness can take many forms.
6. Unexpected difficulties in spite of consistent, evidence-based, targeted intervention.

7. Fluency difficulties – the child may be able to read and even spell, but are they slow? Do they decode every word laboriously? Do they seem to skip chunks of text and fail to get the meaning? Do they struggle with skimming, scanning, summarising? Do they always need more time or is their output lower than you would expect? Do they find continuous prose harder to read than non-fiction (which contains bullet points, diagrams, text boxes, etc.)?
8. Parent reports of difficulties at home – tiredness, reluctance to do homework, dislike of reading/writing.
9. The learner who loses focus and attention easily, often seems off-task, struggles with instructions or is always seeking clarification.
10. A dip in progress in literacy-based subjects later in primary, without an obvious explanation (e.g. reduced attendance).

MYTH: GOOD READERS CAN'T HAVE DYSLEXIA

This is only partially true. Children who read well at different points in their schooling can still have dyslexia. Often there is some underlying difficulty which can be found if reading is thoroughly assessed (e.g. fluency, decoding). Sometimes the underlying difficulties do not cause problems until later on in school. Sometimes dyslexics compensate and learn to read fairly well, but reading is laborious and lacks fluency.

WHEN IT MIGHT NOT BE DYSLEXIA

Point 10 above reminds us to be watchful where there is a dip in progress. It is worth noting that some lesser-known conditions may be mistaken for dyslexia. Examples of this are PANS (paediatric acute-onset neuropsychiatric syndrome) and PANDAS (paediatric autoimmune neuropsychiatric disorders associated with Streptococcal infections), post-infectious conditions that typically occur between the ages of 3 and 13. Among other symptoms (e.g. developing obsessive thoughts and behaviours, tics, anxiety, behaving in a younger way, sensory needs, eating issues and problems sleeping), children with PANS and PANDAS can develop SEND, which can look like dyslexia. In particular, writing is impacted in PANS and PANDAS. More information on how to distinguish between PANS or PANDAS and dyslexic-type writing difficulties can be found in the blog "What happened to Evan's writing?"[15] The message here is that dyslexia is persistent and does not develop suddenly. Any sudden deterioration in literacy skills with no background history of such difficulty is unlikely to be dyslexia and should be investigated.

DYSLEXIA, A DIFFERENT WAY OF THINKING?

Many dyslexic young people report that they process information differently to others. This can be an incredible positive, and many adult entrepreneurs, artists and creatives describe their dyslexia as helping them succeed.

Voices of Dyslexia

"It's the fact that you process information differently. I think that kind of distinction is really positive."

Lisa, parent[16]

In March 2022, the social media platform LinkedIn first introduced "dyslexic thinking" as a skill, defined by Dictionary.com as "an approach to problem solving, assessing information, and learning, often used by people with dyslexia, that involves pattern recognition, spatial reasoning, lateral thinking, and interpersonal communication".[17]

However, in reality, few dyslexics in school have identified this type of thinking in themselves.

MYTH: ALL DYSLEXICS ARE CREATIVE AND VISUAL THINKERS, SEE THE BIGGER PICTURE AND THINK OUTSIDE THE BOX

Only partially true! It's true that many dyslexics are creative and visual, often because they have had to think outside the box, but there is no evidence that these are defining features of dyslexia.[18] Some dyslexics I have worked with were not creative or visually talented at all (though they had other talents).

HOW IS DYSLEXIA IDENTIFIED? IS IT IMPORTANT TO BE DIAGNOSED?

Assessment for dyslexia is carried out by an educational psychologist or a qualified specialist teacher assessor. Diagnosis should involve multiple factors, and the views and experience of the school and parents is a vital part of this process. More information about assessment can be found in Appendix X "How to interpret a diagnostic report".

There are pros and cons to a dyslexia diagnosis. It is expensive, and up to age 7, assessment should focus on identification of needs not a diagnostic label, in order to put appropriate intervention in place.

MYTH: IDENTIFYING DYSLEXIA ENSURES EARLY INTERVENTION

This should not be true! Educators do not need to wait to intervene. In fact, a priority for children below age 8 should be on identifying need and putting support in place, rather than a diagnostic label.

However, from age 8, there are numerous benefits of knowing a child has dyslexia and understanding their learning profile. In the words of a SENCO, who has chosen to remain anonymous:

> *"I'm a big advocate for 'support the needs a child presents with' not waiting for a diagnosis. But with limited SEND training for teachers and TAs, some may lack a deeper understanding of certain needs or the confidence to address them effectively. It shouldn't matter but in reality it often does. Teacher confidence/budget restraints – it all feeds in to what support children get. Sometimes an official diagnosis helps to ensure resources are allocated to a child's needs."*

Perhaps the most poignant advantage of identifying dyslexia is the benefit for the child, in understanding themselves and discovering that they are not "stupid".

Voices of Dyslexia

> *"I am dyslexic. Knowing this has helped me and other people now know the reason I struggle sometimes and how they can help me. The assessor said I did very well in the tests and that I was clever which is something I didn't think I was before."*
>
> Emma, age 11

Dyslexia has come a long way. It has travelled in our perceptions through history from an unknown, mysterious condition in Percy, to a widely accepted, if misunderstood, condition in contemporary popular culture. Today, many people with dyslexia are active in sharing experiences and raising awareness. There is even a popular concept of dyslexia as a "superpower". In Rick Riordan's best-selling Percy Jackson children's books,[19] the main character even has dyslexia (and ADHD) as a product of his divine parenthood! But there is still so far to go in achieving equitable support in schools. My hope is that this book will enable you to join this positive trajectory of history in enabling, equipping and empowering your dyslexic learners to meet their potential.

NOTES

1 Kirby, P. and Snowling, M. (2022). *Dyslexia, a History.* Montreal: McGill-Queens University Press, p. 183.
2 Morgan, W.P. (1896). A Case of Congenital Word Blindness. *British Medical* Journal, *2*(1871), 1378.
3 Carroll, J., Holden, C., Kirby, P., Thompson, P.A. and Snowling, M.J. (2024). Towards a consensus on dyslexia: Findings from a Delphi study. https://osf.io/preprints/osf/tb8mp
4 The Orton Gillingham approach, www.ortonacademy.org
5 Kirby, P. and Snowling, M. (2022). *Dyslexia, a History.* Montreal: McGill-Queens University Press, p.51
6 Elliott, J. (2020). It's Time to be Scientific about Dyslexia. *Reading Research Quarterly*, *55*(51), 561–575.
7 UK House of Lords Judgment (Phelps), https://publications.parliament.uk/pa/ld199900/ldjudgmt/jd000727/phelp-1.htm
8 Rose, J. (2009). Identifying and Teaching Children and Young People with Dyslexia and Literacy Difficulties: An independent report from Sir Jim Rose to the Secretary of State for Children, Schools and Families, June 2009. www.thedyslexia-spldtrust.org.uk/media/downloads/inline/the-rose-report.1294933674.pdf
9 The Delphi method of consultation involves multiple stakeholders in order to gain consensus where there is controversy.
10 Carroll, J., Holden, C., Kirby, P., Thompson, P.A. and Snowling, M.J. (2024). Towards a consensus on dyslexia: Findings from a Delphi study. https://osf.io/preprints/osf/tb8mp
11 Specialist Teacher Assessor Standards Committee (2022). SASC – Format for a Pre-16 Diagnostic Assessment Report for Specific Learning Difficulties. https://sasc.org.uk/media/cbfdeheu/pre-16-years-assessment-report-format-sasc-may-2022.pdf
12 Carroll, J., Holden, C., Kirby, P., Thompson, P.A. and Snowling, M.J. (2024). Towards a consensus on dyslexia: Findings from a Delphi study. https://osf.io/preprints/osf/tb8mp
13 Carroll, J., Holden, C., Kirby, P., Thompson, P.A. and Snowling, M.J. (2024). Towards a consensus on dyslexia: Findings from a Delphi study. https://osf.io/preprints/osf/tb8mp
14 Carroll, J., Holden, C., Kirby, P., Thompson, P.A. and Snowling, M.J. (2024). Towards a consensus on dyslexia: Findings from a Delphi study. https://osf.io/preprints/osf/tb8mp
15 Coope, T. (2024). What Happened to Evan's Writing? https://louiseselbydyslexia.com/what-happened-to-evans-writing

16 Lisa's story on film can be found on the Voices of Dyslexia project page, https://louiseselbydyslexia.com/voices-of-dyslexia-do-you-have-a-story-to-tell
17 Dictionary.com (2024). Dyslexia. www.dictionary.com/browse/dyslexia
18 Carroll, J., Holden, C., Kirby, P., Thompson, P.A. and Snowling, M.J. (2024). Towards a consensus on dyslexia: Findings from a Delphi study. https://osf.io/preprints/osf/tb8mp
19 www.readriordan.com

2

FROM A LEARNER'S PERSPECTIVE

How I do it differently

> "Everybody is a genius. But if you judge a fish by its ability to climb a tree, it will live its whole life believing that it is stupid."
>
> Albert Einstein

Understanding the learning world from the dyslexic learner's point of view is always a very good place to start the adventure of teaching them. In this chapter, we'll look at what it's like to have dyslexia. We'll explore dyslexia as a learning difference, looking at "how I do it differently", considering what's hard for the dyslexic, before looking at strategies to help in Part 2.

DYSLEXIA IS A DIFFERENCE

Dyslexia is a difference in the way the brain learns, and many successful dyslexic adults have found ways to succeed by doing things differently. This discovery is not often made during school days, however. Jamie Oliver, the accomplished chef, broadcaster and author, speaks candidly about his frustration with school.

Voices of Dyslexia

"Something I don't really talk about much is the constant battle I have with words and reading. Without question it is a love hate relationship. In the old days at school it made me very frustrated and resentful about school as an institution and over the years I've come to terms with not learning

DOI: 10.4324/9781003401544-3

the same way as most people not as a failure but an opportunity, an opportunity to look at things differently."

Jamie Oliver[1]

Not every child with dyslexia will find strengths to make them famous, but each one has their talents and deserves to have their voice heard and understood by educators so they can learn not to fail, but to "do it differently" from the start.

WRITING: HOW I DO IT DIFFERENTLY

If you have dyslexia, sometimes thoughts and ideas come to you faster than the words that represent them. When you write, you might have plenty of words in your mind, but these words may come more quickly than you can write them down, or they may come to you in images or mental moves rather than words.

"I quite like writing because I can let my imagination flow. It's like a rainbow of ideas, but I can't get them all on paper and I am really slow."

Callie, age 9

Words and phrases need to be held in mind in order to get them on to the page, but they are easily lost by dyslexics. This is why their spoken language is often better than their writing. Many can excel when using alternative ways of getting their ideas on to paper (e.g. a graphic organiser, writing frame, film, sound recording or picture).

Then there's the spelling. This is challenging for a number of reasons.

"My writing gets all muddled up when I try to spell. I don't use words I want to because I can't spell them. English spellings are weird."

Nathan, age 8

If you have dyslexia, you probably struggle with saying the sounds of a word one at a time in the correct order (phonics), and even if you succeed, you still might forget these sounds when you need to write them down. Many children with dyslexia prefer to recall a word visually than say its sounds. This can work well for many words but not unknown words. It gets even more complicated: some words don't follow phonetic rules (e.g. said, come, where), and some sounds can be spelled in different ways! Which do you use? Is it meet or meat?

It's really common for handwriting to deteriorate when the dyslexic brain is working on all of the elements involved in writing. Moreover, often even by age 7 dyslexics have less physical stamina for writing as they have not had the same level of practice as their peers. Using word processors and assistive technology is often a really useful way of doing it differently for the learner with dyslexia.

READING: CHORE OR CHALLENGE?

Voices of Dyslexia

"I like books, but there are always too many words on a page, and too many pages to read, which is overwhelming."

Esme, age 10

With dyslexia, you may understand complex spoken language, but the same language in writing defeats you. You might have difficulty with looking at letters and saying their sounds, or instantly recalling letter patterns you have seen before (orthograhic skills). Your orthographic skills might be OK, but you have problems when you have to blend them together (phonological skills). Reading can be effortful, slow and tiring. You might struggle to recognise and read word endings (suffixes), making the syntax and meaning of what you read less exact, which then impacts on your comprehension. Maybe you are working so hard to read the individual words that you can't also listen to your reading to check for errors.

Some dyslexics learn to compensate and understand texts extraordinarily well without reading them accurately. These learners' underlying difficulties are often unnoticed in primary school, as they appear to cope well. However, as the level of challenge in texts increases, the cracks in the surface appear and reading difficulties are detected. Some read more slowly than their peers. They will get there, but just need more time. Most dyslexics have to work harder than their peers to hold what they've read in their heads. This means that reading can be tiring, even once the code is cracked.

WORKING MEMORY: THE STICKY NOTES CHALLENGE

Voices of Dyslexia

"I can learn some facts, like times tables, but when I learn other things I forget them, or get muddled."

Jakob, age 9

Working memory is the capacity to hold material in mind and manipulate it as necessary for a brief period. It's like a mental desktop to remember and work with information. It has been compared to a workspace with multiple sticky notes. The sticky notes are not intended to be there forever; they must be used or transferred somewhere more reliable quickly, or they will be forever lost.

Working memory should not be confused with long-term memory. It's possible to remember things that are meaningful and happened a long time ago, while still struggling to hold in mind what's been spoken a few seconds ago.

Voices of Dyslexia

"I am good at remembering some things, like things that just happened, or what I did at the weekend. But when I have to remember something in class, then there is more that comes after the thing I am trying to remember, I forget the first thing. I like to just get going before I forget it."

Arjun, age 9

Individuals with dyslexia often have working memory challenges and need strategies to compensate. I have seen them find all sorts of their own clever techniques to help them hold information in mind, such as visualising, repeating, drawing pictures or even just trying to write quickly, like Arjun:

> *"I like to write very quickly so that I don't forget what I want to say. I don't want to have to worry about spelling and editing."*
>
> Arjun, age 9

However, these clever strategies are difficult to sustain in the busy classroom. Dyslexics work best when the teacher can provide different, less vulnerable methods of providing and storing the information, such as pictures, notes, recordings, movements or written back-up. If information is given meaning, interest, even humour, it's so much easier to hold in mind!

Sometimes a child who has working memory difficulties is thought to be lazy, distracted or a daydreamer. Sometimes children mask so well that teachers don't notice.

FIGURE 2.1

Often, dyslexic learners experience moments of working memory overload. This can feel like overwhelm, confusion, inability to concentrate, and it can even manifest itself physically.

"I know when I need a break in class because my head becomes 'super hot'. At these times it helps me to go to the toilet and wash my face."

Henry, age 9

Excessive demand on working memory can cause fatigue. Often dyslexic learners are exhausted at the end of the school day. Sometimes children have faced challenges before they even arrive at school, as you'll see in the story of Zeb's Day below, illustrated in Figure 2.2 (a colour version is also available as downloadable online Support Material).

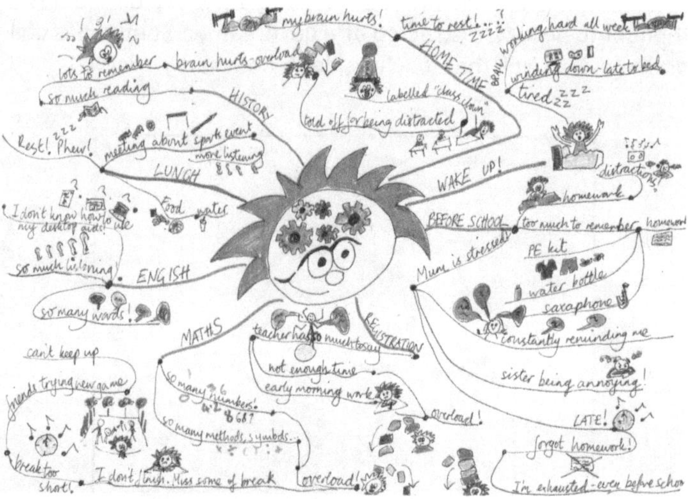

FIGURE 2.2 Zeb's Day

ZEB'S DAY

This is Zeb. Zeb is bright, and he is great in sports and science. But Zeb's day can be exhausting. This is because he struggles with holding words and ideas in his head while working on them at the same time; he has working memory difficulties.

Zeb always wakes up with the alarm; he's tired! Often he's been up later than he should have been the night before – lots of things take him a long time, and he needs his wind-down time too – usually TV or video games. He works hard all week just to keep up with school; it's tough, even though he's capable.

Even before school, Zeb's working memory is put to the test. He didn't get time to finish his homework last night so has to do that, and there's so much distraction! Remembering everything he needs for school is challenging – Zeb doesn't have time now to write lists so it's all in his head. Mum's stressed today too, and they are LATE again. In all the mayhem, Zeb still forgot his homework.

At school, registration has its own challenges. The teacher has so much to tell the class and not enough time to do it. Then there's the early morning work to hold in his head as well. Zeb is in overload and he's feeling the strain already.

Maths. Zeb likes numbers and solving problems but there is so much to hold in his head during maths – not just the numbers but all the steps as well. He usually either forgets the method or the numbers. He is slow because he keeps having to start again, and he makes mistakes.

Zeb doesn't finish his work and misses 5 minutes of break. He really needs that break; when he is in overload, he can't learn any more, and his brain is stretched to the limit. Once he is allowed out, his friends have started a new game and he can't keep up with the rules.

English. Not Zeb's favourite – so many words, so much listening. Zeb has some nice desktop aids that his teacher found for him on a website, but he doesn't really know how to use them. He's struggling just to copy the learning intention from the board.

Lunch time – phew! Time to eat, drink and recharge. Zeb needs this, but he has to go to a meeting about a sports event straight after his lunch. More listening!

After lunch it's history. Zeb loves the debates but can't remember the facts and there's so much reading – he struggles to remember what he has read and to process what it means. He can't read quickly enough, and his brain hurts.

Zeb starts fidgeting. It's not that he wants to be disruptive, but he is exhausted, and his working memory is in overdrive again. This always happens – Zeb has been labelled the class clown and often gets into trouble.

Home time, at last. Zeb is exhausted. Time to rest, or...

To see Zeb's Day on film, visit www.louiseselbydyslexia.com/resources or scan the QR code. (Figure 2.3)

FIGURE 2.3

TASKS IN SCHOOL WHICH PLACE A HIGH DEMAND ON WORKING MEMORY

- Verbal instructions
- Holding procedures in mind while working on them
- Listening tasks
- Holding phonemes in your head while you blend them to make a word
- Remembering a planned sentence/phrase/spelling/number while you write it
- Reading comprehension
- Moving back and forward in a text
- Remembering rules of games - this includes playground games
- Learning information which is random and less attached to meaning (e.g. number facts, figures, dates)
- Information that is provided without structure/organisation - "thought shower"
- Information that is not applied to something meaningful or personal
- New vocabulary and language structures
- Taking notes
- Copying - especially from the board
- Learning new languages
- Remembering verbal messages
- Mental maths

PROCESSING SPEED: I GET THERE, JUST NOT AS QUICKLY!

"Sometimes I just need more time to think about things."

Ahmed, age 11

Some learners with dyslexia have slower processing speed, especially when it comes to verbal information. They get there, just not as quickly! The more that information is conveyed in alternative ways, the easier it will be for your learners with dyslexia to keep up with your speed.

Processing and working memory work together; you need to process information as part of working memory, and in order to process something you need to hold it in mind. Here Jake describes what it's really like to have working memory difficulties and slower processing speed in primary school.

"Sometimes I get mixed up when I have learned something but need to learn something new which is similar but different. I get really muddled. I find it hard when I need to listen to my teacher in lessons, because it's too fast. I forget what has been said. I would really like my teachers to know that I find it very hard when they go too quickly. Then I get frustrated and angry because I can't keep up. When I have to work fast, I get worried, but I try to just tell myself to do it."

Jake, age 9

FIGURE 2.4 Boy Rossie, with permission from Rossie Stone

VISUAL DIFFICULTIES

Visual difficulties are not part of dyslexia and should be diagnosed by an optometrist. However, difficulties with moving and focusing the eyes often occur alongside dyslexia. This impacts both the clarity of what they see on the page and their ability to track text. For these learners, seeing black words on white can be tricky. They might struggle with small or intricate fonts and lines that are too close together. They might struggle to track words across the lines.

Children don't usually know that what they see is not normal, so they are unlikely to tell adults that they are experiencing these difficulties, but there are some signs of visual problems that adults can look out for. When reading or writing, children may frequently blink or rub their eyes, miss lines or word, struggle with copying tasks, sit in an awkward position or cover one eye when reading. They may follow with a finger when beyond the basic level of reading, complain of sore or watery eyes or headaches, or complain of words moving or shimmering on the page. If these difficulties are observed, a regular eye test would be the first port of call, before seeking specialist advice. Sometimes coloured overlays are prescribed by an optometrist, and children report that letters look less blurry and words don't move as much.

Sadly, dyslexia can be a hidden learning difference, and all too often it is overlooked by educators who are struggling with crippling restraints on budgets, time and resources. However, with the right strategies, support and understanding of how learners do it differently, teachers have the power to transform the experience of a child with dyslexia from failure empowerment. Part 2 of this book looks at these strategies. The good news is that by adopting these strategies you'll be teaching all your learners really, really well.

NOTE

1 Devine, K. (2022). It's a constant battle": Jamie Oliver discusses his "frustrating and resentful" childhood with the learning difficulty in a lengthy post. Mail Online, 17 October. www.dailymail.co.uk/tvshowbiz/article-11324257/Jamie-Oliver-details-struggle-dyslexia-discussing-frustrating-school-days.html

Part 2

PRACTICAL STRATEGIES IN THE CLASSROOM

3

STRATEGIES ACROSS THE CURRICULUM

Dyslexia impacts many areas of learning. This chapter will explore some general strategies which can be used across the curriculum. The focus will be on how to remove barriers to learning so that learners with dyslexia succeed. These strategies will be effective for *all* learners, not just those with dyslexia.

TOP TIPS

Before we dig deeper, here are some top tips for teaching learners with dyslexia across the curriculum

1. Be clear where you want the challenge in the lesson to lie.
2. Maximise talking opportunities.
3. Tap into the multi-sensory.
4. Provide back-up with sound recordings.
5. Organise your own delivery.
6. Allow time for review, consolidation and over-learning.
7. Create different ways of recording and assessing ideas.
8. Support working memory and processing speed.
9. Evaluate and be open-minded.

DOI: 10.4324/9781003401544-5

1. BE CLEAR WHERE YOU WANT THE CHALLENGE IN THE LESSON TO LIE

Be clear what your learning objective is and ensure the challenge lies here, not in other areas. So many dyslexic learners struggle with writing the learning objective before a lesson has even started, for example. Ask yourself: Do I need these children to read or write when I am asking them to? Is it an integral part of my learning intention?

2. MAXIMISE TALKING OPPORTUNITIES

Discussion and interaction is often a strength for children with dyslexia, and this can help embed learning or prepare for writing. Finding opportunities to talk can be precious opportunities for them to consolidate learning, and reduce cognitive load from listening.

- **Response partners** work well throughout the primary phase but especially for ages 4-7. Simply stop to talk to a partner during longer periods of listening.
- **"Think Pair Share"** is a great alternative to the "hands up to answer" approach from age 7 up. Learners are first given time to think about what has been said, then discuss, then offer answers. The "think" time allows for slower processors to fully participate.
- **Model the types of sentence you would like your children to use** and encourage learners to repeat the same sentences with their own ideas. These modelled sentences could be written as prompts or recorded as audio files to support speech. For example:
    - In a science lesson for ages 4-7, you might say, "I predict that the car on the oily ramp will go faster. I think this because oil makes me slip." Ask children to repeat the phrases "I predict" and "I think this is because" with their own ideas. Children might respond, "I predict that the car on the sticky ramp will go slower. I think this because when something sticks on my shoe, I can't lift it."
    - In a history lesson for ages 7-11 you might say, "I think this source of evidence is biased against the Vikings.

This is because it uses exaggerated language." Write somewhere visible "I think this source of evidence" and "This is because" for learners to give their own ideas using this structure.

- **Use speaking frames** across the curriculum to scaffold talking and discussion. Most children do not naturally know how to discuss a subject or ask questions of each other. "Talk to a partner about this" can be a challenging question, and if the teacher is not careful, many children will discuss football scores or what's for lunch! Providing a speaking frame can support and help to achieve your desired outcome in the talking. Speaking frames come in many forms; they simply provide questions or prompts to help structure children's talk. Figures 3.1–3.3 are examples of speaking frames across the primary phase.

Speaking Frame

What did you do?

What did you find out?

What would you do differently next time?

FIGURE 3.1 Speaking frame for science (age 4–7)

Speaking Frame

What did Nelson Mandela do that was good?

Did he do anything not so good?

How do you think he influenced life in South Africa?

If you met him today, what would you say to him?

FIGURE 3.2 Speaking frame for history (age 7–11)

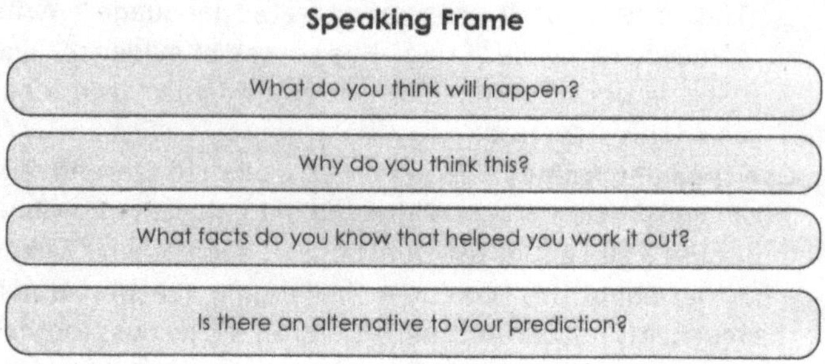

FIGURE 3.3 Speaking frame for science (age 7-11)

3. TAP INTO THE MULTI-SENSORY

Learners with dyslexia usually struggle most with auditory learning, and often work much better with visual and kinaesthetic strategies. In fact, multi-sensory teaching and learning are effective for all children. Use visual aids and pictures, which can even be created quickly by the child, concrete objects as stimulus for discussion, actions, movement, raps, mimes. Figure 3.4 is an example of how visual aids and stories can be used to make facts more meaningful. Dekko Comics offers a range of similar resources.

4. PROVIDE BACK-UP WITH SOUND RECORDINGS

Audio books are popular and readily available commercially and in libraries, and are great to reinforce texts and story work for children in an enjoyable way. For children aged 4-7, sound buttons (simple voice recorders which are easy for children to use by pressing buttons) around the classroom or home with recordings of key information next to written words can be used for sentences, key words, story sequence, instructions, etc. Learners aged 7-11 may still make use of audio files; in addition, headphones could be provided for audio files available on learning platforms or devices.

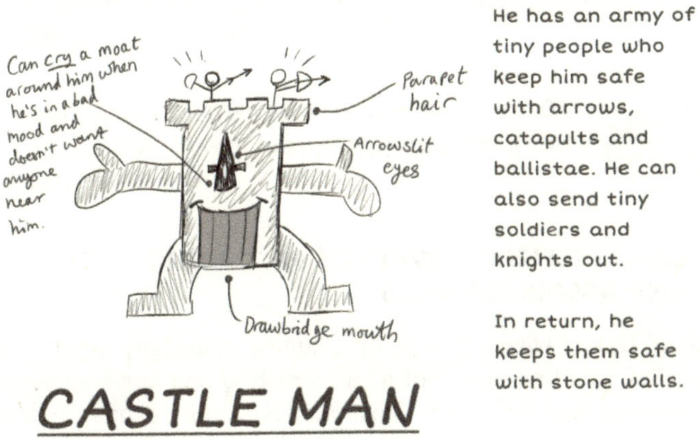

FIGURE 3.4 Castle Man, making facts meaningful, with permission from Rossie Stone

5. ORGANISE YOUR OWN DELIVERY

Sometimes information that is delivered "ad hoc", with thoughts provided as they come, can be problematic for dyslexic learners. It's useful for teacher to organise information in systematic ways and display to learners accordingly, whether this is in a Venn diagram, table, mind map or flow chart. Chunking information in steps is helpful, and providing opportunities for learners to "do" something at each step consolidates.

Voices of Dyslexia

"I find longer instructions hard. It helps when I get to do something at each step."

Amber, aged 10

6. ALLOW TIME FOR REVIEW, CONSOLIDATION AND OVER-LEARNING

Learners with dyslexia can learn, but they might need more opportunities to practise and consolidate. Over-learning can be done in many fun and engaging ways, such as playing games, creating posters, making learning aids and teaching others, and this is an excellent use of home learning time.

Voices of Dyslexia

"Once I know how to do something, I need loads and loads of practice to get the method."

Bailey, age 8

7. CREATE DIFFERENT WAYS OF RECORDING AND ASSESSING IDEAS

Use different ways of recording ideas, especially when the learning intention does not involve writing and spelling: voice recordings, images, mind-maps, podcasts, videos, posters and different kinds of graphic organisers.

Graphic organisers support the process of thinking about and applying information. They provide a visual way to represent verbal ideas, and they support *all* children in getting ideas on to paper and organising those ideas. They are excellent tools for encouraging metacognition as they offer different ways to present, analyse, interpret and organise information.

Examples of graphic organisers:

- Information organising: this can be used across the curriculum. For example, writing about habitats of mini-beasts or English monarchs (Figure 3.5).
- Comparing information: this can be used for any type of comparison – for example, minibeast habitat, towns and cities, school and home, toys, English monarchs (Figure 3.6).
- Structured overview: this can be used to support organising a topic into categories and subheadings across the curriculum. This type of organiser is also useful for planning writing in sections or paragraphs (Figure 3.7).
- Flow diagram: this type of organiser helps with sequencing information (Figure 3.8).
- Frayer model: the Frayer model supports many elements of learning. Place a word, idea or concept in the circle in the middle and interrogate it using the four categories (Figure 3.9.)

	Queen Elizabeth 1st	Queen Victoria
Remembered for..?		
Lived where?		
Transport of the time?		
Reigned for how long?		
School and work?		

FIGURE 3.5 Graphic organiser for organising information

	Queen Elizabeth 1st	Queen Victoria
Remembered for..?		
Lived where?		
Transport of the time?		
Reigned for how long?		
School and work?		

FIGURE 3.6 Graphic organiser for comparing information

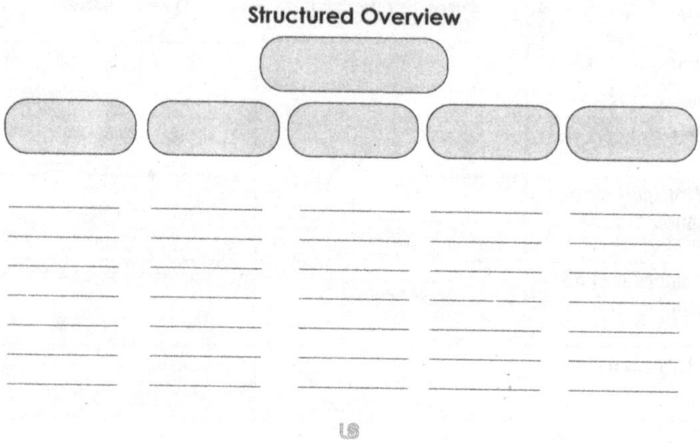

FIGURE 3.7 Organiser – structured overview

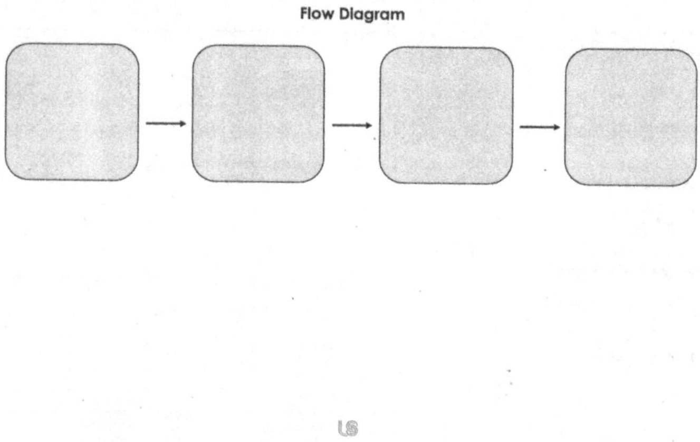

FIGURE 3.8 Organiser – flow diagram

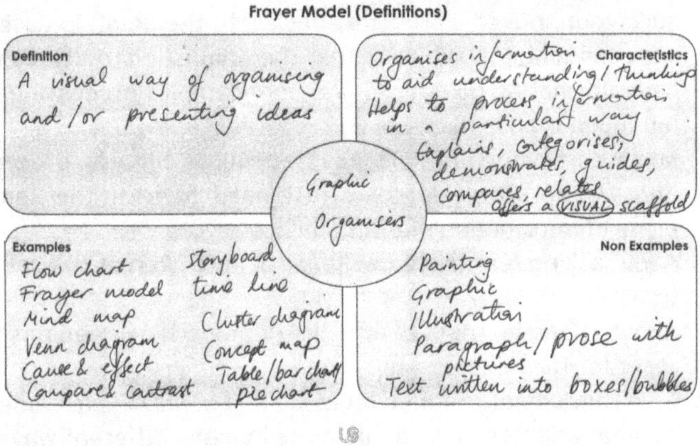

FIGURE 3.9 Organiser - Frayer model

8. SUPPORT WORKING MEMORY AND PROCESSING SPEED

Working memory and processing speed are very closely linked, and strategies to support these areas are similar. Very often, teachers expect children's working memory capacity to be considerably bigger than it is in reality, and it's common for teachers to be unaware of the unnecessary demands that they are placing on working memory in every lesson. Strategies to support working memory and processing speed are as follows:

- Always begin lessons with a review of previous learning, and prioritise the use of plenaries throughout lessons, not just at the end, to support memory.
- Instructions should be clear, concise, given in chunks or steps and repeated if needed. Offer visual and kinaesthetic support for verbal instructions (e.g. show a finished example, walk through or visualise the task, instructions on the board). Consider recording complex instructions on voice recorders or video.

- Evaluate your own use of language when speaking: make sure your spoken words are concise, to the point, in accessible language. Make sure that the linguistic structures of key information do not require more complex processing of language than is necessary.
- Make sure your learners have adequate time to process information. Some learners just need to hear the same piece of information more than once.
- Avoid asking learners to write/work and listen at the same time.
- Avoid asking learners to miss break time - they need this to reset for the next lesson.
- Give random information meaning and context (e.g. names, numbers, facts). This can be done in many different ways - telling stories, adding characters, drawing pictures, making up mnemonics.
- Provide support/scaffolding for verbal group and paired activities - remember it's the verbal load that is vulnerable, so enrich this with kinaesthetic and visual support (e.g. speaking frames, images, notes, written instructions).
- Encourage and support brain breaks/movement breaks.
- Provide visual support and visual aids for orally presented information (e.g. vocabulary banks, examples, memory aids, pictures of a process, diagrams).
- Looks for warning signs of working memory overload in individual learners. This may present as tiredness, distraction, overwhelmed, excessive movement, being off-task, daydreaming, frustration or playing the class clown.
- Be aware of fatigue, especially with home learning tasks - tired brains need recovery time!

9. EVALUATE AND BE OPEN-MINDED

There are no quick fixes for supporting learners with dyslexia, and there is no one-size-fits-all. It's helpful to be open-minded and willing to try different strategies for different children.

Voices of Dyslexia

"Supporting dyslexics is allowing students to try as many strategies as you can think of and things they would like to try. I was gratefully given the opportunity to try all kinds of things. So giving students the opportunities to try things would be best."

Fred, dyslexic, now adult

QUICK WINS

Here are some easy, prep-free ideas for teaching dyslexic learners across the curriculum that you can do straight away.

QUICK WINS
Quick Win 3:
Allow time.

QUICK WINS
Quick Win 4:
Repeat and re-word

QUICK WINS
Quick Win 5:
Do it in chunks!

QUICK WINS
Quick Win 6:
Make up an action
for something verbal.

4

METACOGNITION AND SELF-REGULATED LEARNING

> "Give a man a fish, and you feed him for a day. Teach a man to fish, and you feed him for a lifetime."[1]

Metacognition refers to the strategies we use to monitor or control our thought processes in learning. Self-regulated learning refers to children's ability to independently engage in learning. Metacognition and self-regulation look different at different ages, but should be taught from the beginning of school. These skills are best taught explicitly as part of whole-class teaching;

DOI: 10.4324/9781003401544-6

this is effective teaching for *all* learners, not just those with dyslexia, but if done well, it can be transformative for dyslexics. This chapter explores what metacognition and self-regulated learning are. We'll consider both the challenges for dyslexic learners, and the potential. We'll finish with some strategies and resources.

TOP TIPS

Before we go into details, here are some top tips for teaching metacognition and self-regulated learners

1. Focus on the individual; just as no child is the same, no dyslexic is the same.
2. Focus on empowerment.
3. Focus on the process as well as the product.
4. Be explicit in teaching metacognition; model your thought processes as well.
5. Use multi-sensory strategies (talking, seeing, doing, hearing, even feeling).
6. Look for positives and strengths more than weaknesses and failure.
7. Encourage monitoring and self-regulating from the start.
8. Don't assume that your learners know how to plan, regulate and edit. Teach them!
9. Explicitly help children to activate prior knowledge.

AN AUTHOR'S EXPERIENCE OF METACOGNITION AND SELF-REGULATION

Have you ever written a book? It's a challenging process which requires far more than knowing your material; that's the easy bit! I'll be honest: after the final proofread and submission of my first book, *Morph Mastery*, I swore I would never write again.

Of course, this was short-lived, and here I am now... Truth be told, when I embarked on the task of writing *Morph Mastery*, although I knew the content, I had little idea of the variety of skills I would need.

First, I needed to activate prior knowledge. I needed to know what form this book would take. Where would images and diagrams fit? What would chapters look like? I needed to know my audience: what they knew, needed and would gain from reading this book.

Next, I needed some writing skills and strategies. The book needed structuring into chapters, and each chapter required its own structure. I had a deadline! Dividing my time accordingly was required; this involved setting achievable objectives. Then there was the maximum word count and how to break this down into sections.

As I wrote, monitoring and self-regulation were essential. I needed to find my own voice and hear the text as it sounded to my audience. The skill of self-talk was required, making decisions about content and comparing ideas. Throughout, I needed to manage both the detail and overview, monitor constantly, and check my work for content, length, integrity to audience, accuracy and sense.

Adaptability was crucial. At times, this meant reconsidering how I divided my time (the requirement to home school during the pandemic had a lot to answer for here!), as well as content. I depended not only on having others to talk to, but knowing who would be the best person/group to discuss with each time – whether this was my reliable sounding board, my critical friend, my expert or my potential reader.

In order to achieve all the above, self-knowledge was also required. What would I find easy? Which bits would challenge me most? Needless to say, by submission date I had learned a lot more about my strengths and weaknesses! This has been so much easier the second time round!

Have you noticed how much was involved in addition to the actual content? This level of activating prior knowledge, self-monitoring, self-regulating, adapting and personalising can be compared quite reasonably to learning tasks in the classroom, especially for dyslexic learners, for whom many daily learning tasks may well be as challenging as writing a book.

METACOGNITION AND DYSLEXIA

There is so much to gain by explicitly teaching all children to understand how they learn and to develop their own independent strategies. From the start of formal school, as soon as literacy is formally taught, and sometimes before, dyslexics tend to fail, causing demotivation from the very start. The act of metacognition can reverse this trend: it empowers the learner, it focuses on what the learner does rather than what they can't, it draws attention to strengths as well as weaknesses, it leads to success, and it develops resilience. Dyslexics are often intuitive, interested learners who enjoy understanding how things work and are interested in strategies. Moreover, some learners with dyslexia are more aware than neurotypical learners of how they learn and have worked harder to develop strategies to compensate.

"That history of struggling and struggling and then realising you can do things differently - makes me think there's maybe a different way to do it."

Anna, now adult

However, it's also a bitter reality that most dyslexics have learned more about how they fail than how they succeed by the end of primary school. Educators have a powerful role in redressing this.

"I find remembering things really hard. It's hard to work when there is background noise. I don't like having to do things quickly."

Jacob, age 10

In my assessment work over the years, I have noticed that those who cope better in school are those who are more able to understand and explain how they learn. I am convinced that this has been pivotal in their success.

Voices of Dyslexia

"I can't read out loud and understand. I have to read in my head to process what I read."

Evie, age 9

It's welcome news that all learners with dyslexia display strengths in addition to weaknesses. However, in primary school, reading and spelling take centre stage, and children with dyslexia, whether diagnosed or not, are all too aware of their weaknesses and less aware of their strengths. Learning "how I do it differently" can be pivotal for these learners.

Where metacognition is concerned, there is a risk of focusing on the dyslexia to the detriment of the child. In real terms, the label "dyslexia" and "dyslexia-friendly strategies" are far less important than the process of empowering a child to find strategies for learning that work. As Gavin Reid explains, asking the question "What is the best approach for dyslexic children?" can be unhelpful, as it leads to stereotypical understanding and detracts from the process of supporting individual children with their unique learning profile. Reid writes:

> We know from experience of working with children with dyslexia that the individual differences that surround dyslexia can easily surpass the commonalities, specifically in relation to classroom teaching and particularly as they progress through school.[2]

Therefore, metacognitive strategies, which help all children, whatever their age, help dyslexics even more than adopting the approach of "dyslexia-friendly strategies".

SEVEN IDEAS FOR TEACHING METACOGNITION

The Education Endowment Foundation (EEF) Guidance Report (2021) provides actionable guidance for educators in a seven-step model for explicitly teaching metacognitive strategies.[3] Each step is outlined below, with further actions that teachers can take to specifically support learners with dyslexia. The focus should always be twofold: first, on reducing or removing the individual's specific barriers to learning, which for dyslexics are often spelling, reading, memory, retention and speed; and second, finding and using strengths.

1. ACTIVATING PRIOR KNOWLEDGE

Remember that a learner with dyslexia may need support with verbal work and reading. Visual prompts and photographs of previous work can be helpful. To support memory and retention, activating prior knowledge could be repeated during lessons, not just a quick reminder at the start. "Stop and check" strategies are useful.

2. EXPLICIT STRATEGY INSTRUCTION

Dyslexics will need you to chunk, repeat and reword instructions, and limit the purely verbal. Use pictures to support making connections.

3. MODELLING OF LEARNED STRATEGY

Many children with dyslexia need modelling to be repeated and revisited multiple times; over-learning will be key.

Voices of Dyslexia

"It helps when I practise it a lot in class and go over it again and again."

Natalie, age 8

In addition to modelling what you are doing, talk learners through your thought processes: how you are noticing what you do and how you are adapting. Below is a script of a teacher planning to create a science table. The words which focus on metacognition are in bold:

> First of all, **I need to think how much space I need for this table.** Will it fit on the page? What do I need to put in it? **OK, so I think I need a new page.** Now, how many columns will I need? **How do I work this out?** What will the fields be? Well, **I suppose I'll need** one for the name of the material, and one for different types of properties. **I'm just going to check my results to see** what fits best.

OK, **what do I need to think about** as I draw it? I know it's easy to smudge a pen with a ruler, and I'm left-handed which makes this harder, so I'm going to use a pencil for the lines.

Now, **I think each column needs to look slightly different. I wonder how I will achieve this?** I think I'll use different colours. **Will this work? What's my learning intention?** Oh yes, it's to show different properties of materials. But the first column is just the names of each material, so **those words won't carry as much meaning as the next columns**. The other columns will be more about the properties. **Maybe I could** have one colour for each property. **I think I'll try that and see if it works. I might remember it better too...**

Let's have a look at what I have done. What was my learning intention again? Oh yes, **have I shown** the different properties of the materials? **Let me check with my notes.** Ah, I missed resistance to water; **how can I** add that in now? **Next time I'll need to** be more careful I include everything. **Maybe I could tick things off as I write.**

Now how does it look? **I think I've done it well. It wasn't perfect the first time, but I've learned a new strategy to help me remember next time.**

4. MEMORISATION OF STRATEGY

This is where many dyslexics struggle. They might understand a strategy very well when it is demonstrated, but before they get to doing it, they've needed to listen to something else and have then forgotten!

Voices of Dyslexia

"I would finish the work first out of all of the class but by the time I had to do the homework I couldn't remember how to do it - even if I had done it 30 times in class."

Rachel[4]

Repetition, reminding and modelling in different ways help reduce this effect enormously. Consider providing the strategy as an image, diagram, flow chart or even video. Photographs or voice notes of each step can help. Encourage learners to think about what will help them to remember too, and encourage them to set up their own memory aids.

5. GUIDED PRACTICE

Scaffolding will be essential for learners with dyslexia; gradually releasing control to the learner will support them in achieving your goal. Discuss which steps they can do independently, and provide graphic organisers or writing frames as well as word banks and visual aids. In written tasks, draw attention to keywords, highlight them and write them somewhere clearly, and provide the spellings they need. As you do this, talk to your learners about what helps and why. Talk about, and model, how to use the learning aids you are providing.

6. INDEPENDENT PRACTICE

This will be an important part of the jigsaw for your dyslexic learner, who will need to practise what has been learned, and who will become frustrated if this opportunity is lost. Where possible, allow independent practice immediately after the guidance to minimise the impact of retention problems. Make sure your learners know how to use all the learning aids you give them!

7. STRUCTURED REFLECTION

Most dyslexics feel negative about editing tasks, too often because they focus purely on spotting mistakes and correcting spelling! Why not approach all editing and checking as a structured reflection? Make it not about spelling at all! Look for positives and focus on the learning intention. Use dialogue, but structure it. Encourage learning from others, but ensure that *all* learners know they have something to teach others.

SUPPORTING INDEPENDENT LEARNING STRATEGIES

In primary school, there is a significant focus on learning basic skills: reading, writing and ordering numbers. However, it's really important that from the very start, alongside the teaching of basic skills, children are also taught to plan, monitor and evaluate their own learning. Here are some ideas of how to do this at each stage.

AGE 4–7

- Ask children regularly what they are learning. Make the distinction explicit between what they are doing and what they are learning.
- Involve children in goal and target setting. Talk to them about what they would like to learn in both the short and long term, and encourage them to measure their own progress rather than compare themselves with others.
- Use structured dialogue to encourage monitoring and evaluating - response partners to focus on what we are learning and how we are doing it.
- Build in time for evaluating: What did I do well? What was I good at in this task? What did I find hard? How would I do it differently next time?
- It's vital that from the start children are allowed to talk positively about their weaknesses and mistakes. While this should never be the main focus, it should be modelled that mistakes are OK because they are part of learning.

AGE 7–11

All of the strategies for age 4-7 can be used. In addition:

- Experiment with different types of recording and evaluate their usefulness.
- Discuss different ways to learn and celebrate them; explore different children's strengths and weaknesses.
- Identify three different ways children have learned in each lesson together as a class.
- Challenge children to try different ways to do something.

TEACHING SELF-TALK

This does not usually come automatically to learners, especially those with dyslexia. Sometimes metacognitive self-talk needs explicit teaching and scaffolding. Questions can be provided to scaffold - these could be used individually, in pairs, or even as part of homework activities. Question cards to support this (Figures 4.2, 4.3 and 4.4) are available for download by following the instructions at the front of this book.

NOTE TAKING

The skill of taking notes is not innate! For dyslexics, it can be challenging: it places a high demand on working memory and requires the ability to summarise, prioritise and select words appropriately, as well as spell them. Children are never too young to begin to learn note taking in school. Here are some ideas.

AGE 4–7

- Draw a picture or diagram.
- Use sticky notes, draw a picture or write a word or phrase for each part of a text or poster.
- Choose key words when working in topics or with texts.
- Highlight, underline and mark text as they read/listen.
- Vocalise what they have read/heard in their own words.
- Use talk partners to come up with their own ideas of main points or key words.
- Teach summary - for example, summarising sentences into words, choosing from two possible summaries and discussing which is the best (and why).

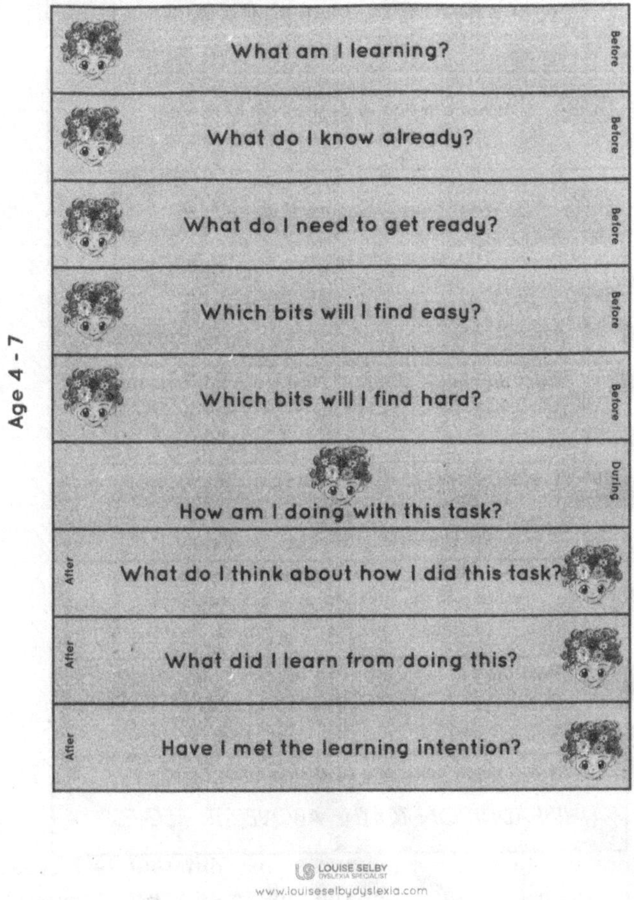

FIGURE 4.2 Metacognitive question card (4-7)

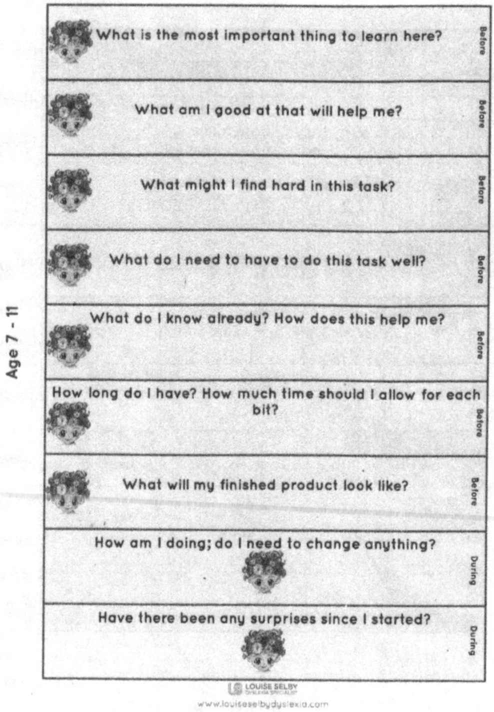

FIGURE 4.3 Metacognitive question cards (7–11)

AGE 7–11 (IN ADDITION TO THE ABOVE STRATEGIES)

- Continue to teach summary across different text types (including visual, auditory and multi-media texts, podcasts, films, presentations, etc.).
- Teach the difference between notes and sentences – looking at features, vocabulary and language structures.
- Use/create pictures with labels as a form of note taking for different types of text and media.
- Talk about the purpose of their notes and what they would like to have them for.

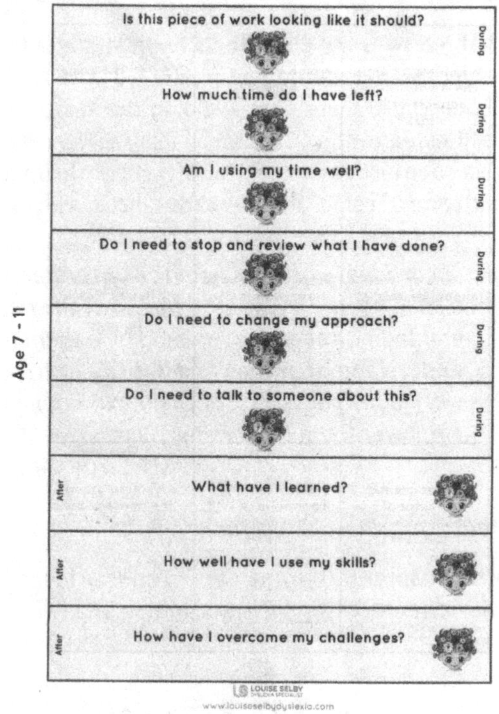

FIGURE 4.4

- Compare different types of notes.
- Experiment with different media for note taking: voice memos, videos, photos, diagrams, graphic organisers, software and applications for mind-mapping.
- Use colour to organise learning into different categories - teach children how to divide texts into different areas and use colour to organise them.
- Consider different subheadings for texts, films, presentations, podcasts, etc.
- Teach effective mind-mapping. There is a useful guide to this on the Dyslexia Scotland website.[5]

SELF-ESTEEM AND SELF-BELIEF

The more that learners are given tools to understand their own learning, the more empowered and motivated they feel. Where dyslexia is concerned, there's no avoiding the fact that it can cause low self-esteem and a sense of failure. However, using metacognitive approaches can help learners begin to understand how they learn and to celebrate their differences. As Gill states:

Voices of Dyslexia

"In an ideal world we would all understand what a child needs. We would value what they bring and their strengths. We would help them to understand what they find difficult or tricky and work out what works for them. We would empower them to learn for themselves."

Gill Carpenter, SENCO[6]

QUICK WINS

We'll finish this chapter with some easy, prep-free ideas for supporting dyslexic learners in - metacognition that you can do straight away.

Quick Win 2:
When you are next modelling a piece of learning, model your thought process as well as the task.

Quick Win 3:
Use your review and plenary to discuss how children learned, not just what they learned.

Quick Win 4:
Use the question prompts in this chapter to ask a metacognitive question in every lesson.

Quick Win 5:
Dedicate children's learning time to create their own learning aids (e.g. word banks, mnemonics, graphic organisers, voice notes, films, pictures).

NOTES

1 Old proverb, thought to be from Lao Tzu, founder of Taoism.
2 Reid, G. (2020). *Dyslexia and Inclusion: Classroom Approaches for Assessment, Teaching and Learning* (3rd ed.). Abingdon: Routledge, p.23.
3 Education Endowment Foundation (2021). Metacognition and Self-Regulated Learning. https://educationendowmentfoundation.org.uk/education-evidence/guidance-reports/metacognition
4 Rachel's story on audio can be found on the Voices of Dyslexia project page, https://louiseselbydyslexia.com/voices-of-dyslexia-do-you-have-a-story-to-tell
5 https://dyslexiascotland.org.uk/leaflets
6 Gill's story on film can be found on the Voices of Dyslexia project page, https://louiseselbydyslexia.com/voices-of-dyslexia-do-you-have-a-story-to-tell.

5

SPELLING

In this chapter, the challenge of spelling is briefly explored, before strategies are offered for support. These include using phonics and syllables, saying words in different ways, looking for parts of words, exploring morphology, and different types of mnemonics.

"My writing gets all muddled up when I try to spell."
Oliver, age 8

Spelling can be the biggest challenge for children with dyslexia. In this chapter, we'll look at some strategies that teachers can use to make it easier.

TOP TIPS

Before we go into details, here are some top tips for supporting spelling

1. Say words as they are spelled, accentuating the syllables or tricky bits.
2. Highlight or trace spellings in different colours, write them in different colours.
3. Look for words within words – for example, there's a **rat** in **separate**.
4. Encourage looking for similarities across words.
5. Make the word using tactile letters. Scramble them, and make it again!

DOI: 10.4324/9781003401544-7

6. Draw shapes around the word.
7. Use visualisation.
8. Make the word into a picture. Learners who can do this themselves are more likely to remember - even if their drawings only make sense to them!
9. Talk about the letters in the word.

PHONOLOGICAL AWARENESS – AN UNDERLYING SKILL FOR SPELLING

It's really useful to use strategies in class which support phonological awareness development as well. Games that can be played in class are as follows:

- I Spy with My Little Eye something that rhymes with/begins with/ends In...
- Robot talk: This encourages children to separate words into constituent syllables or phonemes. For example, to work on syllables, the teacher could say, "What - is - your - dinn - er - choice - Sa - reece?" To which the child responds "I - would - like - yell - ow - please". To work on phonemes (the smallest units of sounds in words), the following might be said by the teacher: "What option would you like for dinner, A - r - a - n?" To which the child responds "R - e - d - please." Combine the speech with movement (e.g. arms moving like a robot) for a multi-sensory experience.
- Encouraging using rhythm and rhyme in learning - for example, make up a rhyme or beat box to learn some facts.
- Regularly segmenting words into their syllables or phonemes (smallest units of sound) – for example, clapping out names of historical figures.
- Read together, focusing on expression.
- For new vocabulary, say the words slowly with emphasised syllables, or make them into a song.
- Ask learners to listen for rhymes, phonemes and syllables in words they are learning to spell – for example, look for syllables in the word "experiment".

SUPPORTING SPELLING WITH PHONICS

Early spelling skills are taught using phonics, and these strategies will also be necessary for some children during Key Stage 2. Phoneme frames on tables throughout the primary phase encourage a culture where learners feel they can use phonic strategies when they need to, even when they are 11! Children are never too old to be encouraged to clap or tap the phonemes in words. Sound mats, including pictures, which display all the possible letter patterns to represent sounds, are also useful through the primary years.

TEACHING CONFUSABLE PHONICS

Many children have difficulty remembering which confusable phonic pattern is correct different words. It's really common for children with dyslexia, who have been taught well using synthetic phonics, to continue to spell phonetically but choose incorrect patterns:

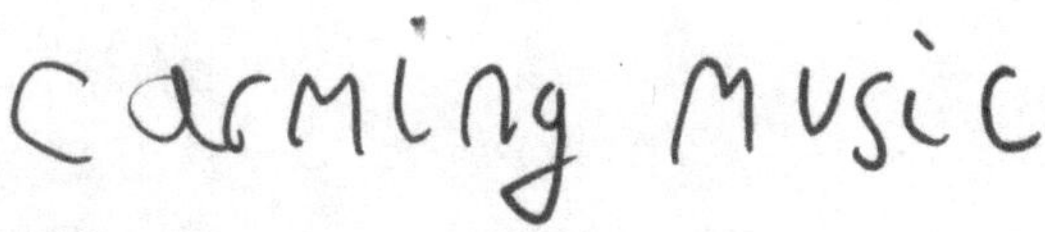

FIGURE 5.1

FIGURES 5.2

Many children who struggle with spelling, whether they have dyslexia or not, need support with knowing which phonic letter pattern to choose, when there are options. Here are some ideas of how to teach this.

1. Use colour coding - each grapheme has a different colour. For example, ay is yellow, ai is green. Learn and write these words in lists to remember them together according to their colour groups (Figure 5.3).
2. Make up stories about words and draw pictures - for example, the snails in the rain on the main plain. Stories like this reduce the random and add meaning, which makes spelling more memorable.
3. Use visualisation strategies to remember confusable spellings. For example:
   A. Choose a word which contains your confusable spelling. For example, the ai in rain, the ee in green, or the igh in light.
   B. Think of this word as a picture (e.g. rain).

FIGURE 5.3 Using colour to support confusable phonic spellings

FIGURE 5.4

FIGURE 5.5

C. While holding this picture in your mind's eye, visualise yourself writing the confusable bit on, or near, your picture in your mind's eye. The confusable bit here is the ai, which could be ay, eigh or a_e.
D. Think of any different picture, one that you can see clearly.
E. Return to your original picture. Check that the tricky spelling is still there. If it isn't, in your mind, write it on or near the picture again. This can be repeated until the word is there each time.

BEYOND PHONICS

Once phonics is mastered, the challenge is to spell longer words. It's useful to help struggling spellers chunk words into syllables. They can do this orally at first, then attempt to spell one syllable at a time (e.g. an/i/mals).

USING MORPHOLOGY (PREFIXES, SUFFIXES AND ROOTS) TO TEACH SPELLINGS

A method of separating words into larger chunks, which is more meaningful than syllables, is using morphology. Morphology refers to units of meaning, known as morphemes, within words, and morphemes can be prefixes, suffixes and roots. It can be helpful to teach learners to look for the root in a word first, then find the suffix and/or prefix.

In the example below, the child has misspelled eaters.

To help him correct this error and remember for next time, his teacher could spend time to separate the word into the root and two suffixes helps with spelling: eat + -er + -s.

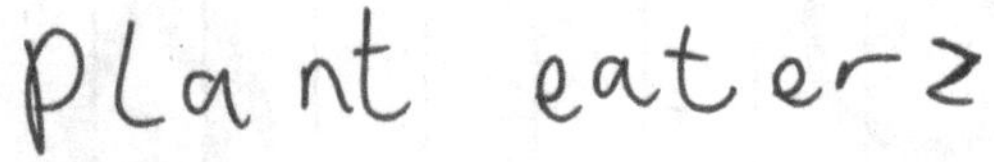

FIGURE 5.6

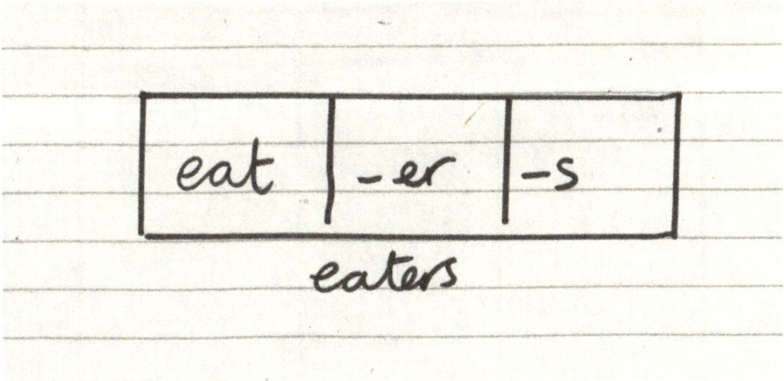

FIGURE 5.7

Morphology can be taught using portals to display words visually, like the ones in Figures 5.8–5.10.[1]

Encouraging children to delve into the bases (roots), prefixes and suffixes can help them to remember spellings, because meaning supports memory. For example:

a. Why do we spell **misspell** with a double **s** but **mistake** with only one **s**? (**mis-** + **spell** = **misspell**, **mis** + **take** = **mistake**)
b. Why is it **jumped** not **jumpt**? (**jump** + **-ed** = **jumped**)
c. Why **business** not **bizness**? (**Business** is a noun that comes from **busy**. **Busy** is the root, **-ness** is the suffix. The y → i rule is applied.)
d. Why do we double the l in **really** when it is single in **dearly**? (**real** + **-ly** = **really, dear** + **-ly** = **dearly**)

LEARNING TO SPELL EXCEPTION WORDS

Some words don't appear to follow the phonic rules; the English language is multi-layered! There are always explanations for spellings, however. Looking at roots and morphemes can help with these (e.g. **people** has a **o** in it because of the word **population**). Talking about spellings and noticing their regular and tricky parts can be helpful. Some exception words can be partially encoded, for example **friend,** which is phonetic apart from the **i**.

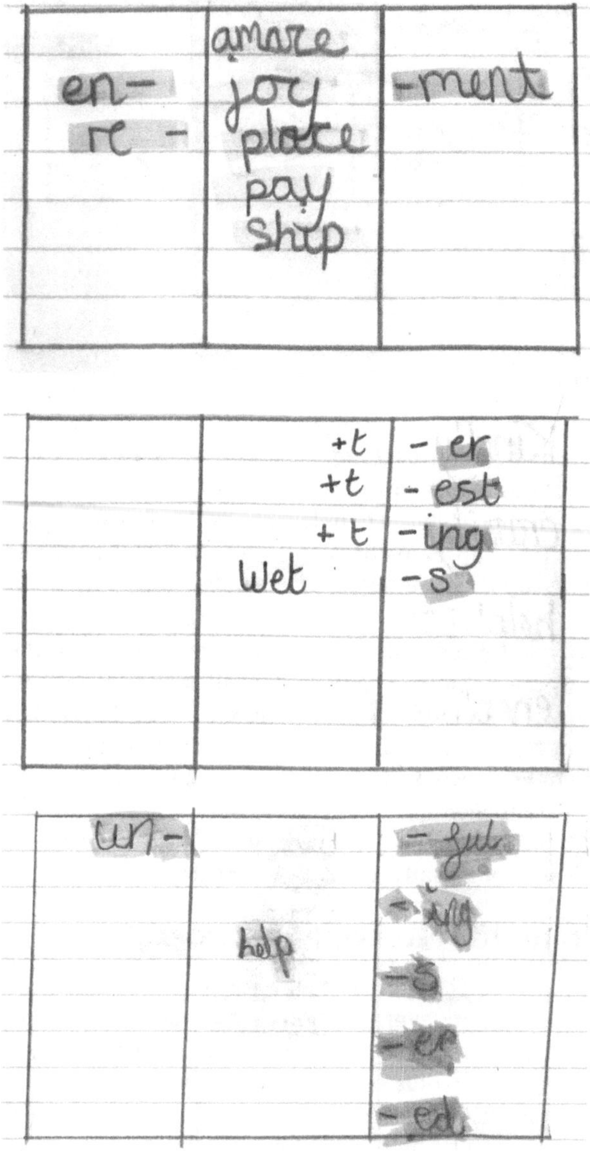

FIGURES 5.8–5.10 Displaying words visually in portals to represent morphemes (prefixes, roots and suffixes)

MNEMONICS

A mnemonic is a memory aid, which usually helps a learner to encode random information so that it is remembered better. Mnemonics can be used to remember letters in words which don't follow spelling and phonic rules. For example:

> **Said = save animals in danger**
> **Because = big elephants can't always use small exits**

Verbal mnemonics like these are relatively easy to create. They work well, but should be approached with caution for children with dyslexia. While verbal mnemonics support the encoding and organising of information by making random letters more meaningful, sometimes they are harder to remember than the spelling itself! They also place some demand on verbal memory, which for many dyslexics would be easier if it were visual.

A good type of mnemonic is both visual and auditory, and, better still, involves movement as well. Creating pictures, posters or cartoons is an effective way to support spelling while reducing cognitive load and maximising memory. Many dyslexics are great at creating these memory aids too. The books by Lidia Stanton offer many excellent examples of this type of mnemonic. Examples are shown in Figure 5.5–5.8 (with permission by Lidia Stanton).

NOTE

1 Selby, L. (2021). *Morph Mastery: A Morphological Intervention for Reading, Spelling and Vocabulary*. Abingdon: Speechmark.

-ould

oh, you (u) little duck

Could you cross the pond? Oh, you little duck.

Would you hurt your legs? Oh, you little duck.

Could I be your friend? Oh, you little duck.

I should help you then. Oh, you lucky duck.

FIGURE 5.11 Mnemonic - "-ould"

FIGURE 5.12 Mnemonic - "want"

FIGURE 5.13 Mnemonic - "watch"

FIGURE 5.14 Mnemonic - "answer"

QUICK WINS

Here are some easy, prep-free ideas for teaching spelling that you can do right away.

QUICK WINS
Quick Win 2:
Do some visualising of tricky spellings.

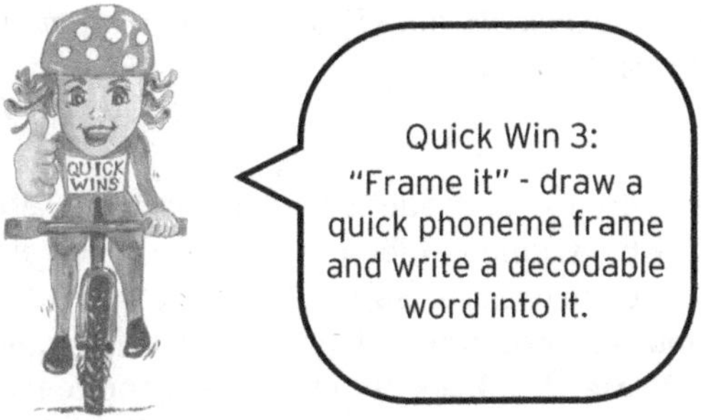
QUICK WINS
Quick Win 3:
"Frame it" - draw a quick phoneme frame and write a decodable word into it.

QUICK WINS
Quick Win 4:
Make a portal and write a word containing a prefix, root and suffix into it - then write some more!

QUICK WINS
Quick Win 5:
Draw a picture: either a visual mnemonic or a shape around a word to help remember it.

6

WRITING

"I find English difficult, especially guided reading and spelling. I like writing stories, especially about horses and animals, but I find it hard to remember what I want to write."

Emily, age 10

Writing is many children's (and adults') nemesis! There are numerous reasons why writing can be difficult, and these are by no means limited to the dyslexic learner. In this chapter, we'll examine why writing is so notoriously hard, and I'll offer some strategies to help. These strategies are just really good teaching, and if adopted will help *all* your learners, not just those who struggle with writing.

TOP TIPS

Before we go into detail, here are some top tips for teaching learners who struggle with writing

1. Provide some opportunities to write for writing's sake.
2. Use alternative methods of recording.
3. Teach for the ***purpose*** of writing, as well as the mechanics, with a focus on the reader.
4. Provide scaffolds, writing frames, spelling aids and graphic organisers.
5. Provide a stimulus for writing, preferably one that is not just text.

DOI: 10.4324/9781003401544-8

6. Provide opportunities to talk as part of the writing process.
7. Ensure that planner sheets are purposeful and not distracting - choose them carefully.
8. Allow sufficient time for slower processors to write and ensure learners get opportunities to finish writing tasks if time is limited - not in play time!
9. Teach positive editing to focus on all aspects of writing, not just spelling and handwriting.
10. Use feedback and positive marking to focus on writing targets, not just spelling.

WHY IS WRITING HARD?

We begin with the "empty page syndrome", when the blank page feels like an insurmountable challenge. Organising ideas into sentences and paragraphs can be difficult: there might be plenty of fantastic ideas, but they can feel like a whirlpool of thoughts. Structuring writing according to text type and audience presents a challenge; knowing how to lay it out, what to write first. Working memory difficulties can mean that holding content in mind while writing it down is problematic; dyslexics can get lost in sentences or forget their ideas easily. If processing speed is reduced, it's hard to keep up, and output might be low, in spite of working hard. Spelling the vocabulary you want to use can be a major source of frustration. You know a great word to use but can't spell it, so you choose easier words instead. Handwriting can also be a barrier to getting your ideas on to paper.

All children with writing difficulties, including those with dyslexia, can feel disengaged from the very start of a writing task, as experience tells them to anticipate negative feedback which seems obsessed with spelling. Editing is also a difficult experience, going back to check what was painful in the first place. In all of this, the process is so challenging that sense of purpose can get lost, and who will read it anyway? What's more, they'll only mark it for spellings, so why bother?

These challenges are general for many children, whether they have a diagnosis of dyslexia or not. The following strategies be used for every child!

TARGET SETTING

It's amazing how often children and teachers are distracted from the intention during the process of writing. Writing analysis and assessment is well-spent time. It helps to set individual writing targets for your struggling writers that are specific, measurable, achievable, realistic and time limited. Discuss targets with the child and refer to them regularly, and focus on the whole process of writing, not just spelling and punctuation.

Example of targets might be:

- Use adjectives to describe/expand nouns.
- Use these conjunctions to join sentences and phrases (insert relevant conjunctions).
- Write a complete sentence that makes sense.
- Check my writing to see if it makes sense.
- Plan a sentence before I write.

TALK FOR WRITING

All children benefit from talking before, during and after writing. It's a really important part of the writing process. However, it's often forgotten, or only done in a tokenistic way. Regular talking opportunities throughout the writing process can help with:

- formulating ideas
- exploring vocabulary
- rehearsing language/sentence structure
- engaging the senses
- faithfulness to purpose
- editing.

Learners with dyslexia also benefit because it removes the stress of spelling and "empty page syndrome". It supports working memory and enables learners to explore ideas without the fear of spelling.

Talking for writing can take place in many forms and may look different for different ages and stages. It can be games as starters to lessons, or scaffolded talking activities to support the language and sentence structures you would like the children to use. It could consist of discussion to support and plan for writing, or peer editing as a discussion activity. Speaking frames can provide questions or prompts to help structure children's talk, therefore enabling them to rehearse the language structures you are looking for. More information about speaking frames is in Chapter 3.

TABLETOP AIDS

Voices of Dyslexia

"I don't like writing at all. I can't get my ideas down. When my teacher gives me some support and a writing planner or grid it really helps."

Phoebe, age 8

Voices of Dyslexia

"Spelling is really hard and I use lots of the same words in my writing because I can't spell longer ones."

Michael, age 8

I remember talking to a child, aged 8, who told me with absolute pride and pleasure about all his tabletop spelling and writing aids. He found each one and showed me them. However, when I asked him how he used them, he didn't have a clue! When considering how to use writing frames, bear in mind all children, especially dyslexic children, need explicit instruction on how to use them.

WRITING MATS

Writing mats have space for the learner to write, with prompts, scaffolds or words on either side. They can be personalised for the learner or class. The prompts can be varied, but common exception words and essential vocabulary are often used. Learners can also be asked to consider which words they might like to use and write them on their own mat in advance. Examples of writing mats are in Figures 6.1-6.4 (also available as online Support Material for download).

FIGURE 6.1 Writing mat

FIGURE 6.2 Writing mat

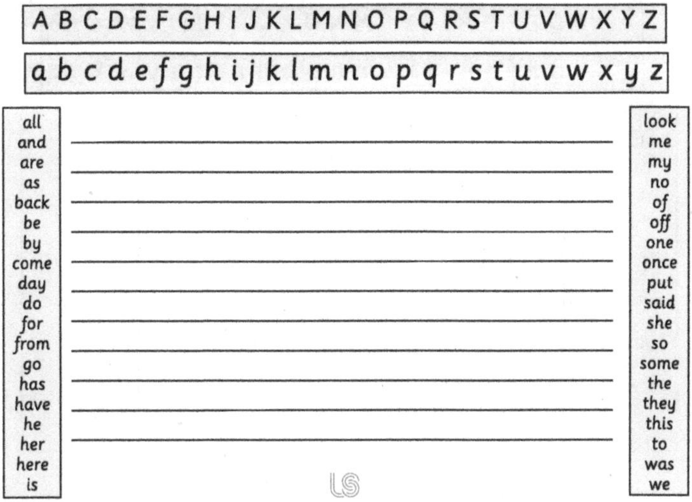

FIGURE 6.3 Writing mat

FIGURE 6.4 Writing mat

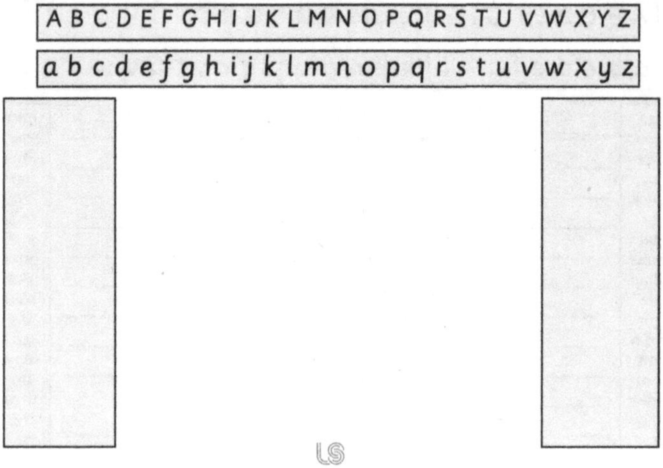

FIGURE 6.5 Blank writing mat

Writing mats can be enlarged and laminated; the learner's book or paper can then be placed in the blank space, or photocopy the mats for the learner to write on the lines. Avoid overloading the learner with too many words.

Mats can also be blank for personalisation as in Figure 6.5.

WORD GRIDS

Word grids are tabletop aids to support spelling. Generally, they consist of key words which are organised in alphabetical order, but they can be personalised. Words which learners might commonly use are chosen. Often these are the common exception words and topic words. Examples are in Figures 6.6–6.8 (and available as online Support Material for download).

a b c d e f g h i j k l m n o p q r s t u v w x y z

Sunday	Monday	Tuesday	Wednesday	Thursday	Friday	Saturday

Aa		Bb	Cc	
all are as		be by	called come	
Dd	Ee	Ff	Gg	
do		for from	go	
Hh		Ii	Jj	Kk
has have he		I if is		
Ll		Mm	Nn	
last love		me my	no	
Oo		Pp	Qq	Rr
of		people		
Ss		Tt	Uu	Vv
said see she		the they to		
Ww		Xx	Yy	Zz
was we who			your you	

January	February	March	April	May	June	July	August
September	October	November	December				

FIGURE 6.6 Word grid

a b c d e f g h i j k l m n o p q r s t u v w x y z

Sunday Monday Tuesday Wednesday Thursday Friday Saturday

Aa		Bb		Cc	
all are	as ask	back be	by	called came	come
Dd	Ee	Ff		Gg	
do don't		for from		go gone	
Hh		Ii		Jj	Kk
has have	he here his	I if	is it's		
Ll		Mm		Nn	
last love		me move	my	no	
Oo		Pp		Qq	Rr
of off	only one	people put			
Ss		Tt		Uu	Vv
said see she	so some	that the them	they this to		very
Ww		Xx		Yy	Zz
was we who	were			your you	

January February March April May June July August
September October November December

FIGURE 6.7 Word grid

a b c d e f g h i j k l m n o p q r s t u v w x y z

Sunday Monday Tuesday Wednesday Thursday Friday Saturday

Aa		Bb		Cc	
all	as	back	blue	called	come
about	ask	be	by	came	could
are	asked	black		children	
Dd	**Ee**	**Ff**		**Gg**	
do	even	for	full	go	
don't		from		gone	
door		friend		green	
Hh		**Ii**		**Jj**	**Kk**
has	help	I	into		kind
have	his	I'm	is		
he	house	if	it's		
here					
Ll		**Mm**		**Nn**	
last		made	move	no	
love		make	Mr		
		me	Mrs		
		most	my		
Oo		**Pp**		**Qq**	**Rr**
of	only	people	push		
off	one	pink	put		
old	orange	pull			
once	our	purple			
Ss		**Tt**		**Uu**	**Vv**
said	she	that	they		very
saw	so	the	this		
says	some	them	too		
see		then	today		
		there	to		
Ww		**Xx**		**Yy**	**Zz**
was	who			yellow	
we	were			your	
where	would			you	
	white				

January February March April May June July August
September October November December

FIGURE 6.8 Word grid

GRAPHIC ORGANISERS AND WRITING FRAMES

Graphic organisers and writing frames reduce "blank empty page" syndrome, and they help the learner to achieve what is intended by the teacher. These can be absolute game changers, if you get them right! More ideas about using graphic organisers (with examples) can be found in Chapter 3.

Writing frames are used specifically to support writing tasks. They are skeletons which provide scaffolding for the writing process. They generally support specific writing outcomes. Writing frames might consist of sentence starters, cloze procedures, questions, boxes with pictures/diagrams, boxes in a sequence, a story mountain - the list goes on. Their role is to support the text type, or structure, of the required piece of writing. Their aim is to remove barriers to writing and to help learners to achieve learning intentions/writing targets without the many barriers that are caused by dyslexia and writing difficulties.

I've seen a lot of writing frames, some more purposeful than others. An effective writing frame supports the learning intention for the task without becoming bogged down in the process. It serves to help the child write what is expected by removing potential barriers. By providing specific support for the learning intention, the quality of writing should improve. Less effective writing frames tend to be more generic, or provide support with an unrelated learning objective. An example would be lines for the child to write on with a picture above, when the child is required to write a report using adverbials. This type of writing frame does not support the specific writing process for that lesson, and adds nothing to the learner's ability to meet the learning intentions.

Questions to consider when creating a writing frame:

- What is the learning intention for the class? How does the writing frame support this?
- What is this child's writing target? What do they need to do to move on?
- What is the barrier to achieving the above?
- What could help to remove this barrier?
- How can I structure the writing frame to ensure that the child achieves the required output?

1	Before my eyes was a		skull	with two	antlers.
2	It stood still,		and		
3	The		skull	stared	back at me.

FIGURE 6.9 Highly structured writing frame to support using adjectives

Figures 6.9–6.11 are examples of structured writing frames with specific learning intentions.

WRITING GAMES

These are an effective and fun way to engage children, which takes the sting out of the mechanical process. If planned carefully, they enhance the multi-sensory opportunities in writing, and ensure learners achieve learning intentions. Games are usually oral. It's a clever way of teaching writing, without asking the children to write! Here's some ideas.

SENTENCE GAMES

1. Copy a sentence. Repeat back the sentence but in different voices – for example, loud, whisper, like a robot. Vary the sentences according to what you are teaching.
2. Innovate on a sentence. For example, "Baa baa black sheep, have you any wool?" could become "Meow meow white cat, have you any milk?" or "They lived in a hole in the trunk of a tree with their Owl Mother" could become "They lived in a nest on a branch of a tree with their Swallow Mother".
3. Quick starters. Use sentence structures you would like children to use and give them one minute to come up with as many endings as they can. The sillier the better! For example:

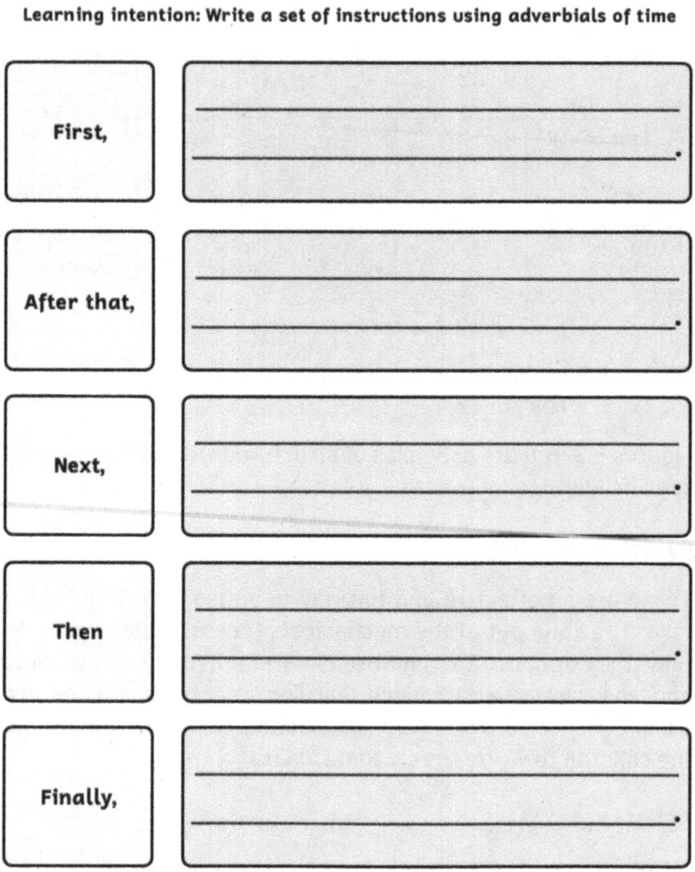

FIGURE 6.10 Writing frame to support using adverbials of time in instructions

- When you have finished...
- After Brian had eaten...
- I would like to argue a case for...

4. Use games to model the sentences you are asking the children to write. For example, a conjunction game: SpongeBob walked to the park... (answers must begin with a chosen conjunction or conjunction from a list provided in advance).

Learning intention: Use conjunctions in persuasion

I would like to tell you about the need for a school journey

[ ]

It is very important for our wellbeing.

School journeys are expensive,

[ ]

The benefits make them well worth the expense.

It's true that some children benefit from excursions with their families,

[ ]

You could argue that this is not the same as school journeys.

In my opinion, the wellbeing of children in our school is at risk

[ ]

we go on a school journey soon.

although,	**because**	**however**	**unless,**

FIGURE 6.11 Writing frame to support using use conjunctions in persuasive writing

5. Finish off incomplete sentences and judge the best/funniest/most interesting, etc.
6. Join two sentences or phrases using a selection of conjunctions - including unsuitable ones. Try different ways to join them.
7. Choose the best sentence from a choice.
8. Guess my conjunction. Give two phrases or sentences that need a conjunction to join them - guess which one it is.
9. Lucky dip. Give each learner or group a card with a word on. These can be conjunctions, adjectives, powerful verbs, adverbials, etc. Then say a sentence or phrase and whoever can prove that their card is the best fit is the winner.

STORY STRUCTURE GAMES

Take turns to say a line or phrase to create a story together. Each person must continue with a conjunction or adverbial, given a choice of conjunctions written on cards. Select a maximum of six conjunctions/adverbials to use. For example:

> Learner 1: Once there was a friendly farmer who
> Learner 2: lived in a cottage. When
> Learner 3: it was summer he worked hard, but
> Learner 4: he was lazy in winter. So
> Here are some conjunctions/adverbials for you to play with!
> who, when, but, because, before, after, if, so, then, while

COHESION AND SEQUENCING GAMES

1. Write sentences on card and cut up the words. In pairs, learners must put them back together again. Extend by omitting one word and asking "What is missing?"
2. Provide copies of texts with some key words deleted. Discuss why they don't make sense and which word could be put in the space.

VOCABULARY GAMES

"Change one word" in a sentence. Write a model sentence on the board. For example: "Slowly, he walked to the door." Take turns to change one word - Quickly, he walked to the door. Quickly, he ran to the door. Quickly, he ran to the exit. Continue until all words have been replaced.

TEACHING EDITING AS A POSITIVE PROCESS

Most children, and not just those with dyslexia, dislike editing! It feels pointless and painful, especially if you struggled with your first draft. One problem is that, commonly in primary schools, editing becomes more of a proofreading exercise - in other words, checking for spellings and punctuation. This can be disheartening for the child with dyslexia as it focuses on their weaknesses, and does not necessarily improve their success against the intended writing outcomes. Editing is more of a thinking and evaluating process than proofreading, which does not even need to involve the mechanical act of writing. Effective editing always focuses more widely and includes the intention for learning - which is rarely spelling and punctuation. Figure 6.12 shows how a positive approach to editing can lead to engagement rather than frustration.

If the distinction between proofreading and editing is made from day one of school, editing can be a positive, enjoyable

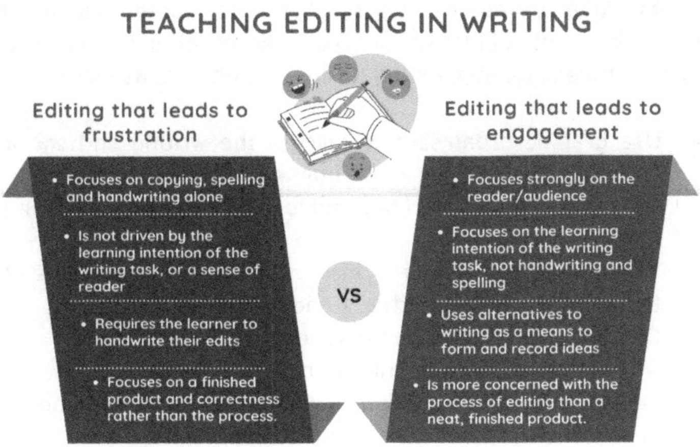

FIGURE 6.12 Teaching editing in writing

experience from the very start. Positive, purposeful editing should be driven by writing targets and learning intentions, *not* a need to make work neater or more correct.

IDEAS FOR SUPPORTING POSITIVE EDITING

Provide focused questions (this could be a speaking frame) for children to consider in order to improve their writing. They could focus on the purpose of writing and audience as well as the mechanics. Examples:

- Have you used some words to help your reader picture what you are writing about?
- Have you used the right words to explain?
- Have you used punctuation?
- Are your words in the right order?
- Do you need to use any other, more interesting words?
- How have you used vocabulary to explain/discuss/describe?
- What do you think helps the reader to enjoy this text?
- Does your writing make sense to the reader?
- What is the impact of your opening?
- How has your punctuation helped the reader to understand?

That is not an exhaustive list! Focus on what your learners need to improve (but not just spelling!) and the intention for learning.

Other ideas for supporting positive editing are as follows:

- Use graphic organisers to discuss the writing and see it from different angles - ask pupils to talk about (or write) their writing in a different graphic organiser (e.g. cause and effect table).
- Talk about your reader - this can include what aspects of the writing help/hinder the reader experience.
- Choose one sentence or phrase to edit against your own writing target/learning intention.
- Edit for the positive - ask children to find positive elements of the writing rather than things to improve.

- Use voice recordings or video to edit. Instead of writing, pupils record their edits.
- Editing competitions. Give children all one text and ask them to make three changes (this can be done in groups or individually). Then choose an "expert reader" to listen to or read the proposed edits of one text and decide on the best, focusing on the reader experience.
- Use colour coding when editing for different things - purple for punctuation, yellow for vocabulary, etc.

EDITING HELPERS

Have different characters/toys who each read and edit for different aspects of writing and edit as a class using them. For example, choose a sloth for sense, a wolf for words, a parrot for punctuation and snake for sentences. Questions for these helpers can then be created according to the piece of writing (Figure 6.13-6.16).

Older children may wish to choose their own characters from cartoons, video games or favourite TV programmes. Depending on the age and stage of the child, extend these helpers' roles. For example:

FIGURE 6.13 Editing helper - Sense Sloth

FIGURE 6.14 Editing helper - Punctuation Parrot

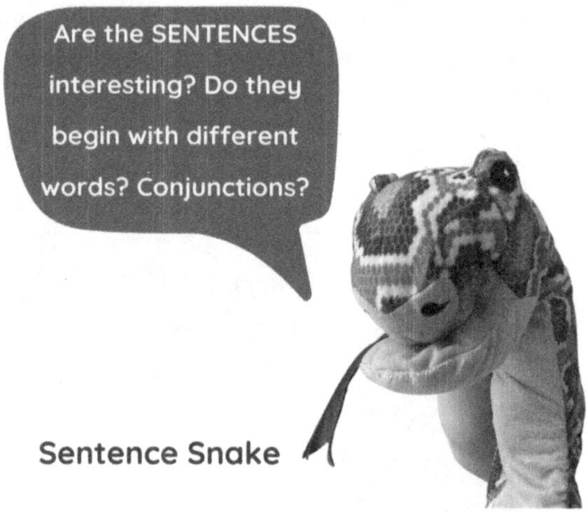

FIGURE 6.15 Editing helper - Sentence Snake

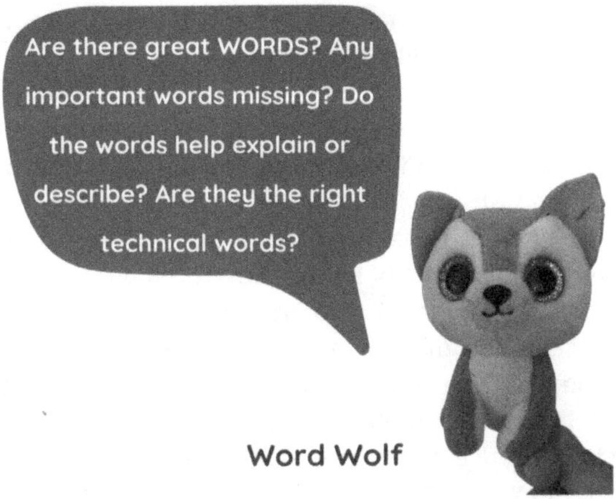

FIGURE 6.16 Editing helper - Word Wolf

- Sentences - varied? Openings interesting? Different lengths for effective and to suit text type?
- Vocabulary - technical vocabulary? Powerful adjectives? Precise nouns? Variety? Impact? Varied verbs?
- Cohesion - makes sense? Sequencing of sentences and phrases? Too many/too few pronouns? Structure of whole text?
- Conjunctions - coordinating and subordinating?
- Adverbials - effective? Describe well? Explain? Fronted?
- Text type - includes main features? Vocabulary/phrasing?
- Punctuation - varied? Effective?

EMERGENT WRITERS

Emergent writers are at the very first steps in learning to write. Even in upper primary school, some dyslexics are still at this stage. A highly structured approach with multi-sensory strategies, combined with step-by-step teaching, can be effective. These learners are likely to need support with developing the actual *concept* of a sentence (as opposed to capital letters and full stops). Some ideas are as follows:

- Repeat back short, memorable sentence in different voices (e.g. loud, whisper, like a robot). Vary the sentences according to what you are teaching.
- Provide card strips with a mix of sentences and non-sentences. The children read them and decide which are sentences, and why.
- Jumbled-up sentence. After reading or writing, cut up a sentence the child already knows into words and arrange back into a sentence. Include the full stop.
- Cut a selection of familiar sentences in half. Match them together. Try this with unfamiliar sentences (but make sure the child is confident in reading them).
- Read a sentence aloud. The children repeat it and count the number of words. Clap/stamp for each word.
- Read short texts with long pauses between each sentence. Ask children to tap the table or raise their hand when there is a pause.
- Provide incomplete sentences (e.g. The little cat was ...) and read aloud. Ask: Are they finished? Do they sound right? Do they make sense? What else can we add to finish it?
- Read a story from a known book together, and clap/tap/raise hand for every full stop or stamp a foot.
- Using sentences from a well-known book, story or text, write out on card and cut each sentence into two parts. Give the cards to pairs of children so they can put them together correctly. Ask them to make sure the sentence makes sense, starts with a capital letter and ends with a full stop. Read the sentences aloud.
- Rainbow sentences. Highlight each sentence in a different colour. Cut up the text into individual sentences. Order these sentences.
- Sentence strips, which are cut up and put together again by the child.
- Co-writing - the child and adult share the writing.
- Pictures with words - matching and sorting activities.

HANDWRITING

Handwriting difficulties are not always present with dyslexia, but some dyslexics have reduced hand stamina, difficulties with letter reversals, fine motor control difficulties and problems forming letters. Here are some ideas to support these different areas.

REDUCED HAND STAMINA

- Provide pencil grips and experiment with different types of pen/pencil.
- Check pencil grip and pressure.
- Take regular breaks.
- Hand-strengthening exercises such as wrist circles, rolling marbles between fingers, squeezing tweezers, scrunching paper (sometimes children enjoy having a personalised "busy box" with this type of activity inside as it also provides a brain break to support cognitive load).

LETTER REVERSALS

- Provide cue cards that work and ensure children know how to use them (Figure 6.17).

Ideally, learners should make their own personalised cue cards, as they are more likely to remember if it is personal. It can be effective to ask children to write their "problem" letters at the top of each page before writing as a reminder. Bear in mind that any cue card should be consistent with the school's handwriting policy. Check your fonts!

LEFT-HANDERS

Writing from left to right is harder: instead of pulling the pen across the paper, left-handers have to push it, which can lead to problems such as a poor pencil grasp, smudged work and arm strain. There are also problems with visibility; a left-hander cannot see what they have just written unless they lift their hand from the page. Left-handers can be supported in various ways:

FIGURE 6.17 Cue card - letter reversals

- Tilt writing paper slightly to the right. Around 45 degrees is usually appropriate.
- Allow the option of using pencil and paper instead of mini-whiteboards.
- Experiment with softer leaded pencils (e.g. 2B), to avoid the grating effect of the pencil as it is pushed across the page by a left-hander.
- Avoid handwriting pens which smudge.
- Experiment with different types of pens and pencils for lefties; there are some which raise the hand slightly to promote visibility and some which support hand grip.
- Sit left-handers on the left side of a table where possible, avoiding the clash of elbows with right-handed peers.
- Allow left-handers to use left-handed rulers, protractors and set squares, which measure from right to left instead of left to right, and therefore increase the left-hander's visibility.

MARKING AND FEEDBACK FOR WRITING

Dyslexic learners often comment on how their work is marked for spellings and little else. Supportive and purposeful marking and feedback, which supports the dyslexic, should:

- be clear about learning intentions and mark accordingly (not just about spellings)
- avoid over-marking for spellings
- ensure the learner can read written feedback - consider using voice notes/verbal feedback
- allocate enough time for the learner to read and respond
- ensure that learners are clear about how they are expected to respond
- focus on the positive more than points to improve and look for strengths
- be consistent.

QUICK WINS

Here are some easy, prep-free ideas for teaching struggling writers in the classroom that you can do straight away.

Quick Win 1:
Use a talking activity strategically.

QUICK WINS
Quick Win 2:
Allow time! Plan when you will allow your slower processors time to finish that is not play time.

QUICK WINS
Quick Win 3:
Play a writing game.

QUICK WINS
Quick Win 4:
Plan at least 2 questions to use for a speaking frame.

QUICK WINS
Quick Win 5:
Plan an editing activity athat does not involve writing.

7

READING

Contrary to popular thought, it is rare for children to learn to read just by looking at books and absorbing language in the environment. Very few learn by osmosis! Every child needs reading to be taught systematically, and this process begins as soon as they enter pre-school. Each child's journey to achieving skilled reading is generally similar, though often not as linear as textbooks would have us believe! In this chapter, we will delve into the different reasons why some children struggle with reading and offer some strategies to help.

TOP TIPS

Before we dig deeper, here are some top tips for teaching reading to learners with dyslexia and reading difficulties

1. Ensure you are using enough books at the right level.
2. Make sure the books for struggling readers are interesting and engaging for their age.
3. Support decoding as well as reading for fluency.
4. Teach active reading (summary, prediction, questioning).
5. Use individual reading aloud for fluency development, not as a substitute for intervention.
6. Allow opportunities to read and re-read class texts, pre-teach these texts to your struggling readers and allow them to re-read and consolidate after a class read.
7. Use audio texts and books.
8. Explicitly teach visualising.

DOI: 10.4324/9781003401544-9

9. Avoid asking children with reading difficulties to read aloud without agreeing it first.
10. Support and train parents, and remember they may also struggle with literacy.

What are the barriers to success in reading?

Traditionally, reading has been thought of as a game of two halves: decoding words and understanding text. Research is increasingly showing us that it is not this simple, especially for struggling readers. Duke and Cartright's Active View of Reading in Figure 7.1 indicates four broad areas of reading (self-regulation, word recognition, bridging processes and language comprehension).

The Active View of Reading reflects the overlap between decoding and language comprehension with what is referred to as "bridging processes", those skills which involve both language comprehension and decoding. This model can be helpful in both identifying specific areas of difficulty within reading and teaching explicitly to address them, as follows.

1. WORD RECOGNITION

Word recognition skills involve decoding, phonological awareness and sight recognition, and these skills are very prominent in the early stages of reading. This is the most common area of challenge for learners with dyslexia. Usually, phonological awareness difficulties are present where dyslexia is diagnosed, and this can impact phonic skills - that is, saying sounds and blending them together (decoding). Some dyslexics also have weaker phonic knowledge - that is, the recall of what sound letter patterns represent. Sight recognition of familiar words is also often very challenging for dyslexic learners. Some dyslexics struggle with words which look similar (e.g. were, where), sound similar (e.g. present, presence) or have similar meanings (e.g. weight, mass).

In early schooling, all children are taught to decode. In England and many other countries, this is mostly taught through

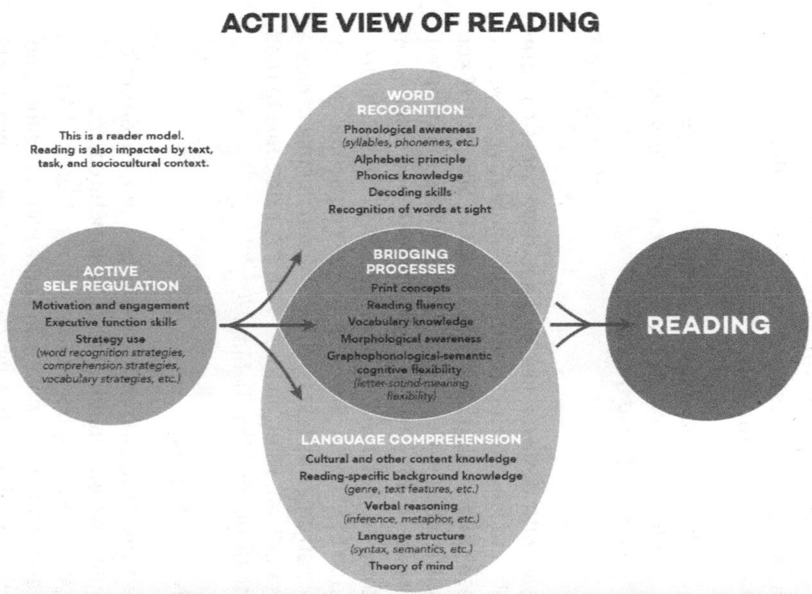

FIGURE 7.1 The Active View of Reading (Duke and Cartwright)[a]

[a] Reprinted from "The science of reading progresses: Communicating advances beyond the Simple View of Reading," by N. K. Duke and K. B. Cartwright, 2021, Reading Research Quarterly, 56(S1), S25–S44. Copyright 2021 Authors. Reprinted with permission. Note. Several wordings in this model are adapted from Scarborough (2001).

systematic synthetic phonics. Learners with dyslexia (undiagnosed in early schooling) may find that high-quality teaching of phonics in class moves too fast. Multiple opportunities for over-learning and embedding what's been taught will be helpful from the start for these children. By upper primary school, children who have dyslexia (which may or may not at this age be diagnosed) often still struggle with phonic decoding (the ability to read a word using phonics), and it's essential that they are taught to read texts accurately and fluently.

"I love stories, especially fantasy. I find reading letters and words very hard. I can understand it but I can't read the words."

Michael, age 8

Some children with dyslexia, like Michael, have great comprehension skills and love stories, but they struggle to read words. Many of these children find alternative ways to access text and mask their difficulties with phonics. Some children find incredible compensatory ways to evaluate, deduce and infer from texts that they cannot read at all accurately. These children sometimes don't fall under the radar of needing additional support, but they struggle as texts get harder, and fluency can be a major problem. "Even when children with dyslexia come to read accurately, their fluency lags behind."[1]

PHONICS INTERVENTION

If learners are still struggling with phonics by age 7, children may need more intensive intervention which is structured, multi-sensory and provides lots of opportunities for over-learning. A focus on blending and segmenting skills using pure units of sound (phonemes) will be essential. A film which shows how to pronounce these sounds can be accessed using the QR code below.[2]

Sentences and texts to practise reading phonemes that have been taught should not include words that are too difficult for the learner. Use phoneme frames and sound buttons (counters

Articulation of sounds

FIGURE 7.2

which represent each phoneme) to practise blending and play simple games like Bingo, Snap and Tic Tac Toe to practise (there are some games templates available for download by following the access instructions at the start of this book). Remember that children with dyslexia need much repetition and over-learning at this age.

2. LANGUAGE COMPREHENSION

Language comprehension involves vocabulary knowledge, background knowledge, language structures, literacy knowledge and verbal reasoning. It's common for learners with dyslexia to display good language comprehension, and for their weakness to be more word related. However learners who have lacked exposure to print may have also missed out on some background knowledge required to access texts. This is more likely if the learner has some speech and language delay as well. Vocabulary can be a strength for learners with dyslexia, but again, where exposure to print has been reduced, it may not have developed as expected, or there may be gaps. Language structures, grammar and syntax can be an area of challenge for dyslexics. If verbal reasoning is impaired, the learner may struggle with interpreting deeper texts, such as poetry, and understanding sophisticated language structures, such as metaphor.

STRATEGIES FOR TEACHING READING COMPREHENSION

Encourage learners to ask questions themselves. It's worth scaffolding this with questions on cards. There are some cards available in colour for download by following the instructions at the front of this book (Figure 7.3-7.4).

- Encourage and explicitly teach visualising. Many children need help to picture what they read and/or hear in their heads. Younger learners can be taught to picture words and sentences as they are spoken; move towards stories and texts for older children.
- Use speaking frames. These can be a great way to structure conversation about a text and help children to understand it as they read. More information about speaking frames can be found in Chapter 3.

What do you think will happen..?
Who is the main character? What kind of character is s/he?
Where is the text set? What kind of place is it?
When is the story set? How do you know?
Why did ____?
What if____?
What would you have done____?
What examples of interesting vocabulary can you find?
Does the text have a climax? Which part, and why?

FIGURE 7.3 Reading comprehension questions (4-7)

- Teach prediction (Figure 7.5). Prediction involves activating prior knowledge, using inference, reading for meaning and looking ahead and processing what's already been read. It can be part of monitoring understanding mid-reading, or preparing for the next section. Younger children may focus on predicting events, but as the children progress through school, there can be a focus on what the author intends, what is coming next or what the conclusion might be. There is no wrong answer when predicting! Learners should be trained to give reasons for their predictions. To be taught effectively, prediction usually needs scaffolding, and dyslexic learners will benefit from working step by step to predict. Encouragement to consider author intent and what is already known supports prediction.

What information does this text give you about...?
What have you learned on this page?
What else would you like to know?
Did you like this text? Why/why not?
What made this interesting?
Is there a word that helps you understand___?
Who is the text for?

FIGURE 7.4 Reading comprehension questions (7–11)

Encourage questioning and active clarification before, during and after reading texts. Children could write down words they don't understand while reading so they can clarify them with a teacher or using a dictionary. They could be asked to highlight specific things when reading - for example, highlight the full stops, phonic patterns, conjunctions, morphemes.

- Teach children how to summarise. Summary is a difficult, but important, skill to learn, not just for comprehension, but for future note taking and study skills. Summarising usually needs explicit teaching, however, especially for learners with dyslexia. It is the skill of drawing out the main points from a text and involves distinguishing between detail and overview, prioritising what is important and understanding the main point of a text. Like prediction, summarising can be done during the reading, not necessarily after it. It is useful to scaffold summary by giving the reader options to choose from. Summary can be taught at different levels throughout the primary stage. Some ideas to teach summary, of varying difficulty, are as follows:
    - Draw a picture of what you have heard or read.
    - Say a word about what you have heard.
    - Choose from a selection of words to summarise what you have read.
    - Give a choice of two summaries and learners choose which is the best.
    - Choose one word which best summarises a sentence - from a choice of words.
    - As above but choose your own word.
    - Choose an image or emoji to summarise (given a selection).
    - Ask children to draw a text as you read it - you'll need to select the text for this activity carefully.

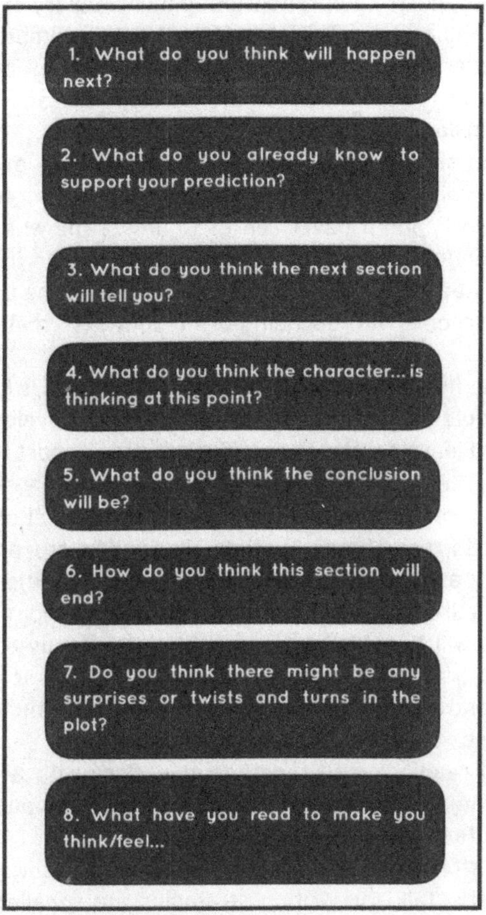

FIGURE 7.5 Questions to support prediction

3. BRIDGING PROCESSES

These are the processes involved in bridging from decoding skills to making sense of texts. Morphology, which refers to the smallest units of meaning within words (prefixes, roots and suffixes), supports comprehension and vocabulary skills, while swift vocabulary recall is fundamental for comprehension. Some readers with dyslexia find the early stages of reading very difficult to master, and some develop fantastic language comprehension skills while struggling to decode. Their comprehension skills jump ahead, but the frustration and lack of fluency remains. Some dyslexics appear to read extremely well by guesswork, and it never ceases to amaze me when assessing children just how much meaning they can gain from a text with poor decoding skills. It's essential at any stage that learners who struggle with decoding are taught systematically and explicitly.

Reading fluency can be a problem for dyslexics, who usually need multiple opportunities to re-read texts to develop fluency and embed learning. Here are a few ideas to support this:

- In class, celebrate, praise and encourage the act of re-reading texts, sometimes multiple times. You are developing fluency and providing over-learning opportunities as well. Some learners will gain from simply reading and re-reading; others will benefit from a change in the focus each time: phrasing and expression can be the focus for at least one read, and using different types of voices each time can add interest.
- Choral reading: read together as a class with a focus on phrasing and expression, exaggerate phrasing and emphasise different words.
- Learn stories off by heart and create actions for them (Pie Corbett's Talk for Writing strategies are excellent[3]). This strategy works especially well for ages 4-7.
- Provide opportunities for reading texts before the lesson. This is effective for readers who are able to decode texts well, but who just need time than most in order to understand (learners with processing speed and working memory difficulties fit into this category).
- Pre-teach main vocabulary, terminology and tricky words in text.

4. ACTIVE SELF-REGULATION

It's common for learners with dyslexia to struggle with some elements of executive function, especially working memory. This impacts comprehension. Motivation and engagement for reading can be high at the start of primary school, but learners with dyslexia often become demotivated and disengaged by the end, due to the amount of effort they have put in to achieve the same results, or worse, than their peers. Often they lack strategies to tackle text and struggle with inference. For fluent reading to take place with good understanding, the reader must become increasingly strategic; self-monitoring, summarising, interpreting, decoding new vocabulary and internalising the reading voice (i.e. not reading aloud) are all aspects of this.

SUPPORTING ACTIVE SELF-REGULATION IN CLASS READING

- Pause and ask. Stop at different points and spot check understanding with a question. The children can ask these questions themselves
- Ask children to read texts in mixed ability pairs. Remember when grouping that the child with dyslexia may have oral language much better than his/her reading level and match with others accordingly
- Avoid asking children with reading difficulties to read text aloud in turn; they generally spend the time practising their bit, which detracts from their comprehension

Voices of Dyslexia

"When I do need to read aloud, I read my bit ahead to get the words ready."

Lena, age 9

- Provide recordings of important/key texts for children. They can listen to them in advance with headphones and at home, and listen to them as they read.
- If possible, allow dyslexic learners to read the text with an adult – in a group, guided reading or one to one, in advance of a whole-class read, or to reinforce a whole-class read.

- Read the text to the class first, asking them to listen and visualise it.
- Teach children how to use text-to-speech software/apps/facilities. It's good practice to use these for all children and evaluate their usefulness as a class.
- (Younger readers) Repeated reading - adult reads, children repeat. This can be done in different voices or speeds to support noticing patterns and use of expression.
- Read small chunks together, then children read the same text to each other, in pairs.

INDIVIDUAL READING SUPPORT

One-to-one reading with an adult, or older reading mentor, is enormously valuable at any age. Lots of the strategies above can be used to support decoding and develop fluency and self-regulation. However, one-to-one reading should never replace explicit teaching of how to decode. If children are struggling with word recognition by age 6 or 7, it's important that systematic intervention is considered.

One of the most important factors in supporting children with reading difficulties is the choice of text. All children should be encouraged to explore stories and text through sharing books and being read to, and children's choices are important. However, for reading instruction to take place effectively, the text that a child is asked to read needs to be readable for that child.

Voices of Dyslexia

"Having books at the right level really helps me. I don't mind reading these aloud, but I hate reading difficult texts aloud."

Lena, age 9

Ensure learners' ability to accurately read words matches the books they are given to read. In England, children aged 4-7 are currently expected to be reading decodable books. These are books which follow the progression of phonics teaching adopted by the school; learners should not be given books containing words they are not yet able to decode. For children with reading difficulties, this will be vital, as phonics often is much harder and decoding laborious. The challenge with decodable books is that dyslexics need multiple over-learning opportunities. Check that you have enough books to allow for multiple opportunities to practise at each level before moving on, and if you don't, this will need addressing.

When phonics is secure, children sometimes are moved on to different-levelled reading schemes. Again, beware of schemes which move them too quickly. Some book-levelling schemes move children through book levels according to their comprehension rather than accuracy of reading words. This can be problematic for children with dyslexia, like Michael, who mask their decoding difficulties with good comprehension skills. Ensure that these children are moved up book levels according to their ability to accurately read text, or level of phonics, rather than just comprehension.

A good rule for readability of a book is that at least 90 per cent of words in a text should be read accurately by the child. This avoids frustration and supports teaching. Often this comes as a surprise to parents, who want their children to be challenged, and are less aware of the importance of developing fluency.

From age 7, the gap between your dyslexic learners' chronological age and reading level may be wide. Sometimes these children are asked to read the same books that they read when they were 5. This needs addressing; children have a right to enjoy books at their reading level, and there are plenty of these available for purchase. Invest in books that are pitched at older learners who struggle with reading. There are many widely available "high interest low level" books which are pitched for learners who read at a lower level than their age. Some publishers are listed in the resources section.

PARENTS

Voices of Dyslexia

"Supporting a child with dyslexia can be very difficult, trying to keep their confidence going whilst their friends around them are picking up

> *books and just being able to read without seeming to put any effort in. And I know from Oliver's perspective, he would come home from school and we would do reading practice and he would say to me, 'I'm a rubbish reader. Mummy.' It's very hard to try to explain to your child who's only 8 that he's not a rubbish reader. He just has to learn how to read in a different way. And throughout all this, Oliver has shown so much perseverance, and all credit to him because he is now starting to read independently. It is great to hear him giggling away reading a book."*
>
> Pippa[4]

The role of parents in supporting struggling readers is immense, and yet they usually receive no training! Moreover, some parents have literacy difficulties too; dyslexia runs in families! Sadly, there is unnecessary shame around this, and parents in this situation don't often reach out for help. Most parents don't know how phonics and reading are taught in school. Many don't understand the book-levelling systems used in school. All parents want to see their child progress, but not as many know what this looks like.

TIPS TO HELP PARENTS WITH READING WITH THEIR CHILD

1. Educate: teach parents how phonics is taught and how the pure sounds are articulated (see the QR code above for a link to the "Articulation of sounds" film).
2. Empathise and support: remember and acknowledge that it can be difficult for parents to see their children struggle.

3. Explain what progress looks like to avoid misunderstanding about moving up book levels.
4. Guide parents how to ask comprehension questions of their child – for example, provide sample questions.
5. Explain why it's important for children to read, re-read and read texts again.
6. Offer support for parents who may struggle with their own literacy and signpost to adult literacy services.
7. Celebrate successes and communicate regularly.

QUICK WINS

Here are some easy, prep-free ideas for supporting struggling readers that you can do straight away.

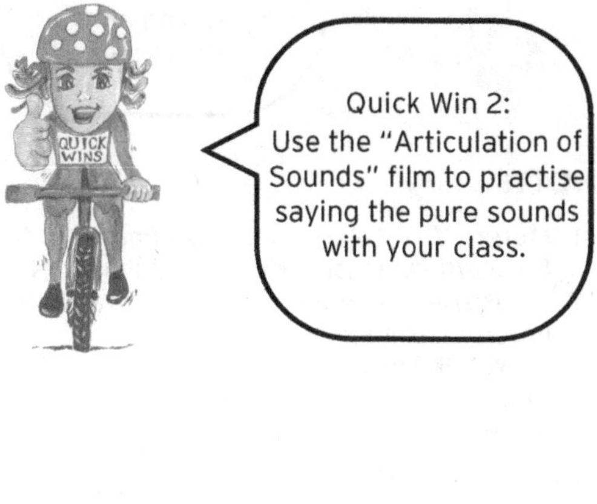

NOTES

1 Muter, V. (2021). *Understanding and Supporting Literacy Difficulties*. Jessica Kingsley Publishers, p.189.
2 https://louiseselbydyslexia.com/lessons/free-video-articulation-of-sounds
3 www.talk4writing.com
4 Pippa's story on film can be found on the Voices of Dyslexia project page

8

ASSISTIVE TECHNOLOGY

Voices of Dyslexia

"Eva really enjoys the text help feature on the lap-top and really gets involved with her creative mind and making up loads of interesting stories."[1]

Lisa, parent

Voices of Dyslexia

"We had touch typing that was put in place at primary school which has been absolutely invaluable. So before my daughter left primary school, she could touch type fluently, which has been an absolute godsend for her."

Louise, parent of dyslexic

Assistive technology can be revolutionary for children with dyslexia, as the demands of reading and writing increase. There is so much available, which is now more accessible than ever, but where should we start? In this chapter, we'll explore some different types of assistive technology and how it can be used to support dyslexic learners in the classroom. Schools vary greatly in the availability to children of computers, devices, operating systems and software. With this in mind, we'll look at some general principles and focus on free and low-cost assistive technology.

TIPS

TOP TIPS

Before we dig deeper, here are some tips for using assistive technology with dyslexic learners

DOI: 10.4324/9781003401544-10

1. Start using assistive technology from the beginning of school in age-appropriate ways.
2. Make the most of inbuilt free assistive technology on school computers and devices.
3. Use technology to record key information that might be forgotten (e.g. instructions).
4. Teach children to evaluate pros and cons of different types of assistive technology.
5. Inform parents about how to use inbuilt free assistive technology.
6. Ensure children have basic keyboard skills by the end of primary school.

It is never too early to begin thinking about using technology to support learning. Often, when I recommend typing and assistive technology for children aged 10 upwards, I find their computer skills are under-developed and they need to start with basics. All children benefit from practising using computers and devices (beyond internet and video games) from a young age.

ASSISTIVE TECHNOLOGY TO SUPPORT READING

- Audio books (use from any age) – these are available free from libraries or cheaply from www.listening-books.org.uk.
- Computer readers (text-to-speech/read aloud) – some of these are internet dependent, some stand alone without the internet. They allow you to see text and hear it being read, using computer generated voices, at the same time. There are many free versions of these. Devices all have built-in, free text-to-speech options. From age 4, children can start to understand how text-to-speech works by playing with devices and software. By age 9, they should then be ready to start using it to support reading of longer texts.

- Display control - changes the font, font size, colour and spacing of text on screens. From age 4, children can be taught to use these features and start to evaluate how they help.
- Reader pens (age 10+) - these are portable devices which scan text and read it aloud. They have different features, depending on the type you purchase and your budget. Some scan text and send it to a computer, some have voice recording features, and some have dictionaries. Reader pens support independence and enable children to access class texts across the curriculum. Advantages are that they are portable and discreet, and versions of them can be used later on in formal examinations.

ASSISTIVE TECHNOLOGY TO SUPPORT WRITING

- Keyboards and touchscreens can relieve the stress involved in writing.
- Spellcheck amd grammar check - these should never replace teaching spelling, but can be a useful aid for struggling writers who want to focus on their ideas for longer writing tasks. Be cautious with the use of spellcheck and grammar check, as they can also lead to perfectionism and over-focusing on spelling and grammar. Also, spellcheck does not correct spellings which could be correct but in a different context (e.g. the meet on the barbecue is tasty). Spellcheck and grammar check should never replace good editing skills!
- Dictation (speech-to-text) - as you speak, the words appear on the screen. Again, many free options are available. More sophisticated versions are available commercially and offer more features. Some dictation software can convert audio recordings into digital text.
- Word prediction (predictive text) suggests correct spellings of words after only a few letters are typed. Some use word banks (commonly used words in a topic area).
- Text-to-speech (computer readers/reader pens) can be used for editing and monitoring writing, as well as reading (see

above). This is invaluable for the dyslexic who often finds it very hard to read back their own work.

- Digital thesaurus - either online thesauri or inbuilt synonyms can be extremely helpful for children who struggle with writing.

SUGGESTED PROGRESSION IN USING ASSISTIVE TECHNOLOGY

AGE 4–7

- Use audio books and teach children to find and listen to them.
- Encourage use of audio books/library audio apps at home.
- Teach children how to use inbuilt text-to-speech and speech-to-text features.
- Use audio recordings in the learning environment using voice recorders.
- Teach children to use voice record features themselves as a way of recording ideas and communicating.
- Record instructions, vocabulary and key information on audio or video for learners to access.
- Invest in recordable whiteboards.
- Teach keyboard skills.

AGE 7-11

- Teach children how to highlight and play back text using inbuilt features on websites and text documents.
- Provide text-to-speech opportunities for children with reading difficulties to support reading of main class texts.
- Train parents in using text-to-speech and speech-to-text.
- Teach touch typing. Teach touch typing (the skill of typing without having to look at the keys). For dyslexics, touch typing programs need to be highly structured and move at a steady pace. A "little and often" approach is best.
- Use text-to-speech features to support editing where children have typed their writing.
- Teach children how to use spellcheck, including the disadvantages.

- Record instructions, key information and maths procedures on audio or video.

ONLINE LEARNING PLATFORMS

"Using assistive technology is second nature to us. We record in so many different ways and upload on to the learning platform. When it comes to dyslexia, the learning platform is our biggest win."

Mollie Keiley, SENCO, St Joseph and St Bede RC Primary School

Learning platforms can dramatically improve inclusive practice while reducing teacher workload. For the dyslexic, the learning platform's capacity for multi-sensory support – for example, with films of maths procedures that can be watched again and again, images of what homework should look like for those who forget, or verbal instructions on audio file – means children can independently hear instructions again without the embarrassment of having to ask. Learning platforms also allow easy uploading of alternative methods of recording (e.g. pictures, work on whiteboards, films), and the fact that children can upload these themselves makes this independent for the child. In addition, children can submit homework without losing it on the way to school!

USING CHATGPT AND ARTIFICIAL INTELLIGENCE (AI)

The phenomenon of "just Google it", bringing easy access to a world of information without effort, has been superseded by "just ChatGPT it". Using AI, children can not only find out what they want, but create, adapt and re-shape whatever they want, whether this is via ChatGPT or using AI-informed software for graphics, films and music. There are some great benefits, but AI comes with a health warning! It's really important to be aware that while ChatGPT can be a useful tool, this is still an emerging area.

ADVANTAGES OF AI

- AI can help children get started on tasks, avoid "empty page syndrome" and gain ideas for structuring writing as well as content.
- Video-making programs support alternative methods of recording. Children can very easily incorporate text with film, sound and images, relieving the load from the verbal memory and the problems with writing.
- Graphic design programs support children in putting ideas into posters and infographics. Weaker writers can produce work which looks fantastic and enables them to communicate their ideas in a different way to writing text.
- Music-making programs enable all learners to explore creativity.

DISADVANTAGES OF AI

- There is a danger that types of AI such as ChatGPT eliminate the thinking and grappling processes that take place before a final product can exist. As Alex Quigley writes, "Pupils need to grapple with new words - write them down, struggle with them, look them up, use them badly, get feedback, and then use them better. They need to write flawed stories filled with errors and clumsy expression, thereby learning how to edit and adapt their writing, so that they ultimately find their own unique voice."[2]
- Dyslexics are often creative; be careful that the use of AI does not reduce their creativity.
- The vital process of planning, drafting and organising learning is at risk of not being engrained if children rely on AI.
- Children using graphic design programs become focused on presentation and the finished product, and look for perfection in presentation rather than content.
- AI finds its information from popular theory via the internet which may not always be factual or correct; children need to learn discerning skills.

QUICK WINS

Here are some easy, prep-free ideas for using assistive technology that you can do straight away.

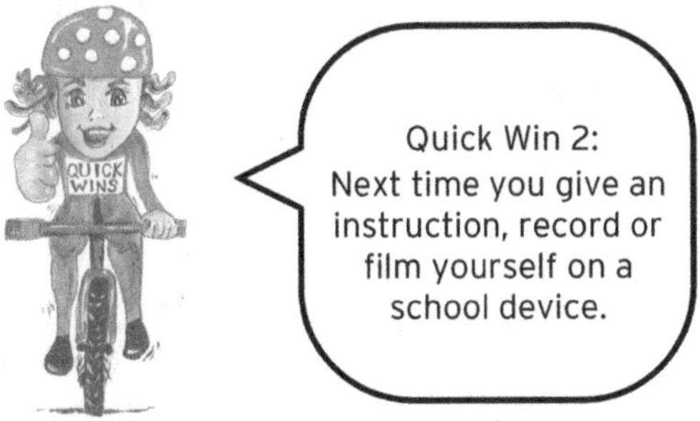

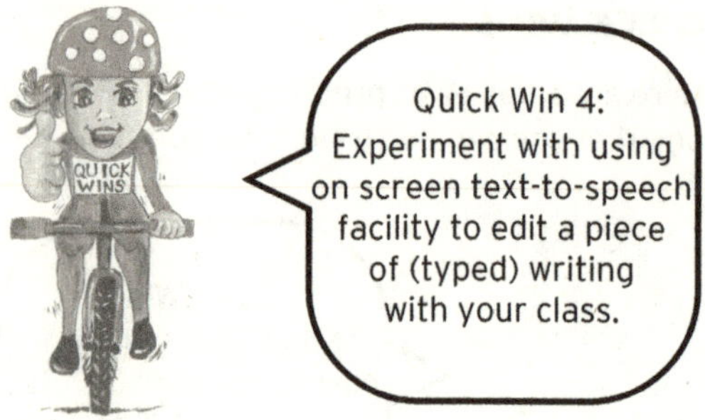

NOTES

1 Lisa's story can be found on film on the Voices of Dyslexia project page, https://louiseselbydyslexia.com/voices-of-dyslexia-do-you-have-a-story-to-tell
2 Quigley, A. (2023). Why might ChatGPT damage learning? https://alexquigley.co.uk/why-might-chatgpt-damage-learning

9

MATHS

Voices of Dyslexia

"The thing I want the most help with is maths."
Logan, age 9

Logan was a child I assessed and found to have dyslexia. Spelling and writing are really hard for him, but what he wants the most help with is maths. Does Logan have dyscalculia as well? Probably not; his basic number sense is fine, and he can estimate and compare numbers. In my assessment work, I often hear stories similar to Logan's from children who have dyslexia but experience difficulties with maths as well. In this chapter, we'll look at how dyslexia impacts maths and consider some strategies for support. These strategies are in fact effective for all learners in your class.

TIPS

TOP TIPS

Before we dig deeper, here are some top tips for teaching learners with dyslexia who struggle with maths

1. Do oral counting every day.
2. Make abstract information meaningful and therefore memorable.
3. Support with vocabulary, and use colour coding consistently across the school.
4. Provide concrete materials, visuals and memory aids.

DOI: 10.4324/9781003401544-11

5. Allow multiple opportunities for over-learning, be prepared to repeat things, allow time.
6. Provide reading support.
7. Pre-teach to enable access.
8. Minimise the need to work purely orally.

DYSCALCULIA OR DYSLEXIA?

Difficulties with maths can be caused by any (and in some cases, more than one) of the following three areas:

1. Dyscalculia, a specific learning difficulty which causes a problem with sense of number.
2. Other specific learning difficulties (e.g. dyslexia), which do not directly impact sense of number, but which can have an impact upon mathematics learning.
3. General learning difficulties, medical conditions, environmental factors (e.g. attendance issues), maths anxiety or gaps in teaching leading to weak foundations.

Both dyscalculia and dyslexia impact maths, so it can be useful to consider some key similarities and differences between maths difficulties relating to dyscalculia and dyslexia (Figure 9.1).

Dyscalculia impacts basic number sense. Children with dyscalculia usually have severe difficulties with aspects of arithmetic and calculation. They lack an intuitive understanding of relationships between numbers and therefore struggle with comparison and understanding size of numbers. They struggle to generalise what they have learned, such as a method of calculation, and therefore they tend to rely on memorising procedures, which they may not understand, and rote learning. There is much more information about dyscalculia and how to support in Judy Hornigold's book in this series.[1]

Dyslexia, on the other hand, does not impact basic number sense. It is not known to cause difficulty with understanding magnitude of numbers or relationships between them. In fact, often dyslexics can estimate and compare numbers well, and

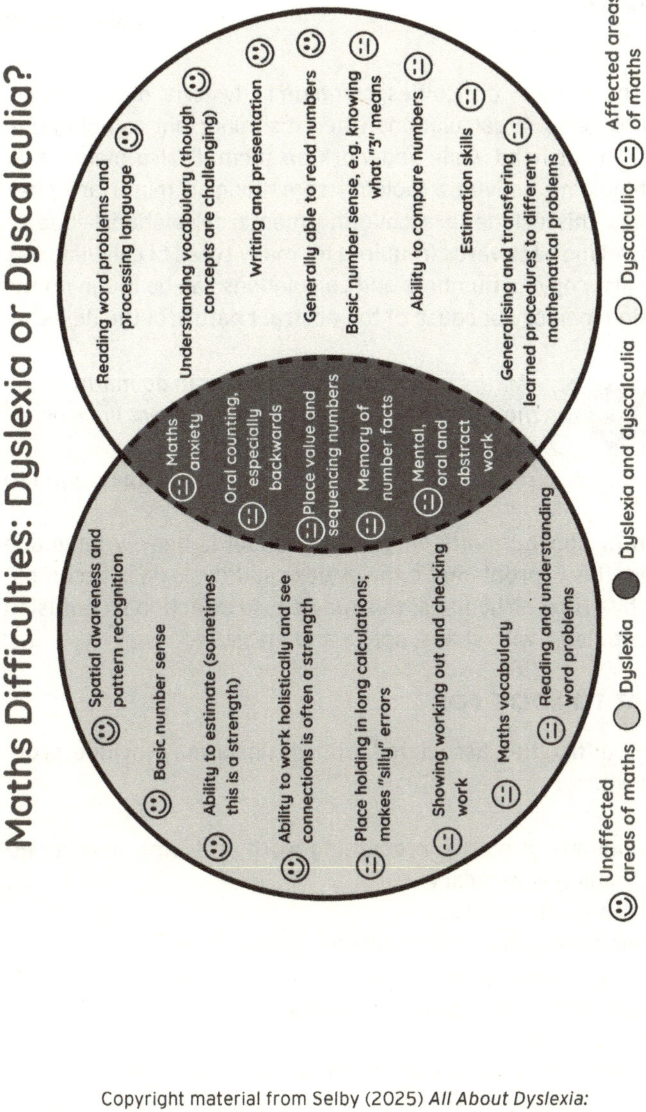

FIGURE 9.1 Dyscalculia and dyslexia

they work intuitively. However, the underlying cognitive difficulties that accompany dyslexia can impact mathematical skills.

Voices of Dyslexia

"I really struggle with maths. The teacher says things but I can't follow them and I get lost."

Caroline, age 8

Working memory difficulties, common in dyslexia, mean that it's hard to perform calculations when it's important to hold numbers in your head while you work on them. It also means that place-holding activities (holding something in mind) are challenging. This includes oral counting, mental calculation, sequencing, working backwards (required for many types of calculations). Even just copying numbers and calculations can be tough on the working memory because of the abstract nature of the digits.

Voices of Dyslexia

"Maths Is hard. Everyone else can do maths In their heads but I need to use numbers lines or hundred squares."

James, aged 10

Much of applied maths in primary school is heavily language based; this is problematic for dyslexics. If dyslexia is accompanied by visual difficulties, this may cause directional confusion and problems with shape, space and measure.

WHAT TO LOOK FOR

Maths difficulties associated with dyslexia may include problems with:

- language of maths, processing word problems, and understanding vocabulary
- sequencing numbers
- remembering number facts and procedures
- reading long numbers, especially decimal points
- getting lost in longer calculations
- mental maths work
- oral counting, especially when working backwards

- time and measurement
- directional confusion which can impact geometry and shape work
- reading words and questions
- "silly" errors due to difficulty with reading, writing and checking work
- making their own notes, showing their working out and presenting their work legibly
- confusing digits and placing them in the wrong order when reading or writing numbers
- fractions and decimals
- algebra
- using mathematical equipment accurately and correctly (e.g. calculators, protractors and set squares).

"Sometimes I read the question well but I get the numbers mixed up, so I read 1, 0, 8 but say 180."
Brandon, age 11

While there are differences between types of maths difficulties resulting from dyscalculia and those caused by dyslexia, there are also some overlaps. Both involve difficulties with memory, oral counting and ordering numbers. Both mean that learners are likely to struggle with the abstract, and to work best with concrete learning and multiple over-learning opportunities. Both are often the cause of maths anxiety at some point in their schooling (and sometimes beyond).

Whatever the cause of a learner's maths difficulties, what matters most is accurate assessment of where each learner's difficulties lie, so that helpful strategies can be put in place. The rest of this chapter will cover some ideas and strategies in brief for supporting maths difficulties associated with dyslexia.

1. PRACTISE ORAL COUNTING DAILY

Backwards can be much harder for dyslexics! Make it visual and kinaesthetic. Use manipulatives to show counting steps (e.g. cusinenaire, multi-link, numicon, number square).

2. SCAFFOLD THE ABSTRACT

Working memory difficulties associated with dyslexia can be supported by reducing abstract concepts. Maths concepts are best learned using a pattern of concrete-pictorial-abstract (CPA); this model works at any age and is very supportive of working memory difficulties. Develop visual aids for tricky learning. For example, Figure 9.2 (also online) shows number lines to support with the confusion between "teen" and "ty" numbers, a common area of confusion for dyslexics.

3. SUPPORT READING OF WORDS AND SYMBOLS

Dyslexic readers will often paraphrase text they read and still understand; this is not possible with maths. For example, "What is the volume of" could be read as "what is the value of", or "diameter" could be read as "diagram". It benefits all children to go through reading vocabulary before and during a task. Colour-code mathematical symbols and keep this consistent throughout the school. Word charts and tabletop aids can be provided to help -for example the tabletop pyramids in Figures 9.3 and 9.4. Colour versions of these are available for download as online Support Material.

4. SUPPORT PLACE VALUE

Dyslexics can be confused by the position and value of numbers, especially when multiplying or dividing numbers by 10, 100 or 1000. Use manipulatives and visual reminders.

5. SUPPORT WITH WORD PROBLEMS

In addition to the strategies in point 3, teach children to visualise or play a mental movie of a word problem (Figures 9.5–9.7).

6. NUMBER FACTS (E.G. TIMES TABLES, NUMBER BONDS)

Dyslexic learners are likely to need considerable support with learning and memorising number facts. Use concrete apparatus, play over-learning games and provide visual aids.

FIGURE 9.2 Teens and teacups

7. MENTAL MATHS

Mental maths is challenging for learners with dyslexia. Support with visual aids and movement, allow learners to record questions and listen back to them, teach learners to listen out for numbers and key words and make a note of them, chunk longer calculations, repeat and reword. Minimising the necessity to work purely in the oral domain is a big help!

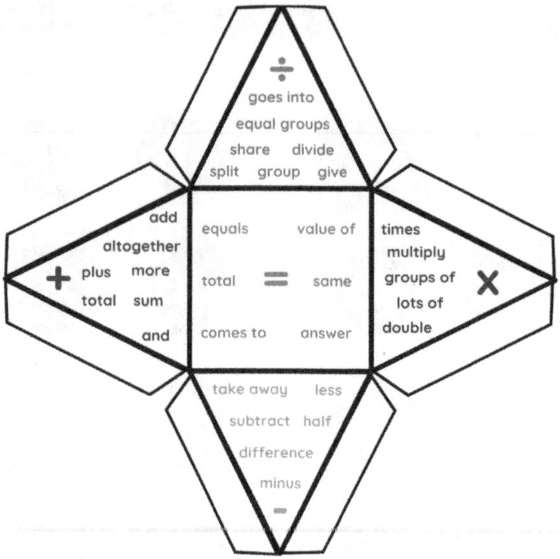

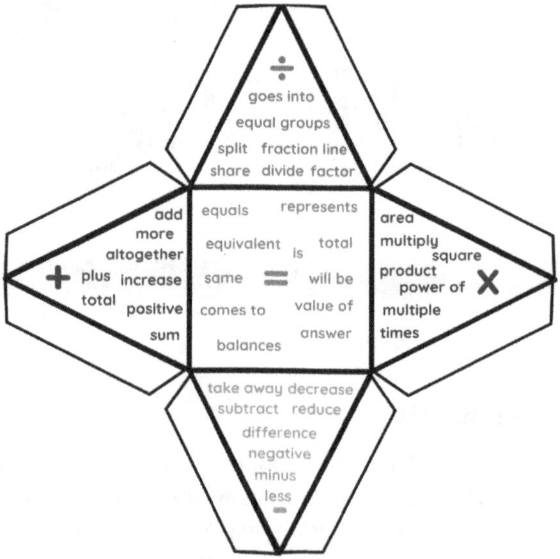

FIGURES 9.3 AND 9.4 Tabletop pyramids using colour coding to support mathematical vocabulary

Take your time to picture Stanley with his 8 cats.

Then picture "me" with 2 cats.

Spend time picturing what the cats look like, and what Stanley and "me" look like. Compare the size of the group of 8 cats with the group of 2 cats.

Take your time to picture Stanley giving me 5 cats, one at a time. Count the cats as they are being given to me. Look at the cats that are left over. You may not know the number of cats here but think about the size of these left over cats.

Now picture Stanley with the leftover cats. Look at the size of this group, compared to the group that both people have.

FIGURE 9.5 Visualise word problems in steps

To help with remembering larger numbers within word problems, visualise the image with a number on it. The more detail you can give to your visulaising, e.g. colour, size, background, the more likely you are to remember it.

FIGURE 9.6 Visualising with larger numbers

Picture the place and the people in the word problem. Check that you have 2 adults and 2 children. Spend time picturing what they are wearing and doing to help you remember.

Think about the prices in the problem. Picture the prices next to each person. At this point it's fine to check what the numbers look like. Picture your numbers in a colour you like and make them clear.

Now do your calculation of the adult tickets. Keep your picture in mind; remember you have two adults. Next, do the same for the children's prices. Picture your totals next to your people, and again, make them stand out in a way that you can remember.

Now you can complete your calculation.

FIGURE 9.7 Teaching visualising of complex problems step by step

8. VISUAL PROBLEMS AND DIRECTIONAL CONFUSION

Use line guides, tracking aids and L-shaped cards. Allow left-handers to use left-handed rulers and protractors. Allow plenty of space for working out.

QUICK WINS

Here are some easy, prep-free ideas for supporting dyslexics with maths that you can do right away.

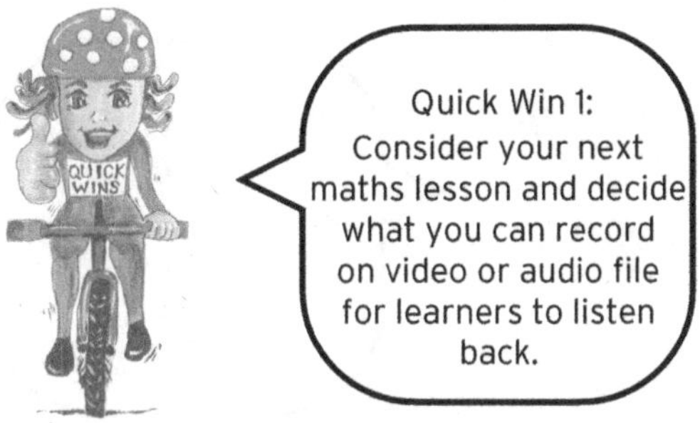

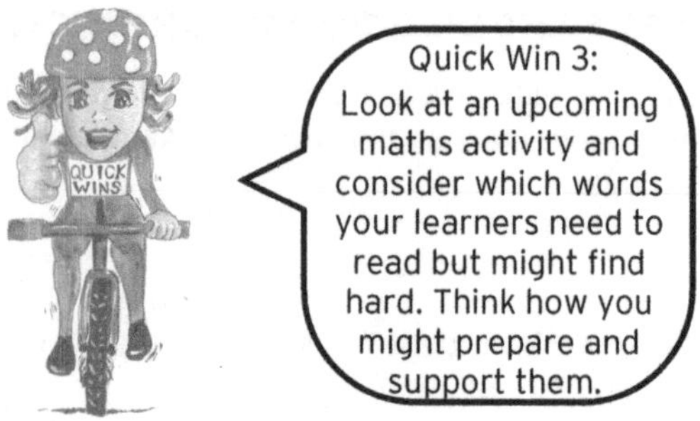

NOTE

1 Hornigold, J. (2024). *All About Dyscalculia: A Practical Guide for Primary Teachers*. Abingdon: Routledge.

Part 3

WHOLE-SCHOOL APPROACH

10

CREATING A DYSLEXIA-FRIENDLY SCHOOL CULTURE

TIPS **TOP TIPS**

Before we dig deeper, here are some top tips for developing an inclusive school culture with reference to dyslexia

1. Evaluate what deeply held beliefs and underlying assumptions drive your practice.
2. Avoid the "dyslexia-friendly" tick-box exercise.
3. Listen to your learners and be prepared to adapt.
4. Promote a culture of celebrating difference and finding strengths.
5. Be aware of the impact of language and interaction.
6. Remember that you are preparing learners for a future world.
7. Regularly assess and review your inclusive practice.

Culture runs deep into the heart of a collective set of values and beliefs, which are bigger than a vision statement. School culture drives what *really* happens in school. It can be a positive influence, but often when considering inclusion, it can be more of a ball and chain! No matter how inclusive the school's published values are, within the cultural core there are always assumptions that are held without challenge, and some of these can be the opposite of inclusive.

The cultural iceberg model[1] can be a useful analogy (Figure 10.1). Beliefs and values sit near the surface. Some are

DOI: 10.4324/9781003401544-13

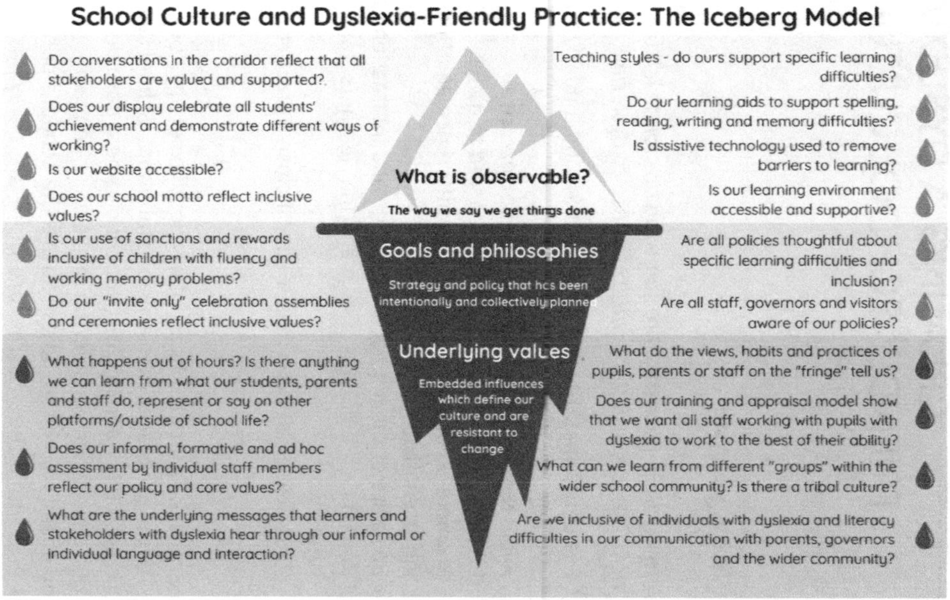

FIGURE 10.1 The cultural iceberg: questions to consider around dyslexia

observable, for example the school motto, while some are only revealed by looking under the surface, for example school policies and teaching strategies.

"When I went to see the SENCO because I was worried my son might have dyslexia and was falling behind, she told me all classes are dyslexia-friendly and they meet his needs through dyslexia-friendly strategies. But I don't know what those strategies are, and I feel fobbed off. As far as I can tell, they have done nothing extra for him and he isn't making progress."

Primrose, parent

Primrose's son's school was aware of dyslexia-friendly strategies and had adopted some in classrooms and whole-school practice. However, her comments reveal that dyslexia-friendly provision was perhaps superficial at her son's school.

Developing inclusive school culture which makes a lasting impact involves walking the walk, not just talking the talk. It doesn't sit in a theoretical vacuum, but is a product of high-quality daily interactions. I regularly hear from individuals with dyslexia, teachers and parents that no matter how much they implement strategies to support and enable, the whole education culture still promotes unhelpful messages. This is highlighted by Sobel and Alston:

> There is an underlying belief among some teachers, TAs and even children that it is not "proper" learning unless it is demonstrated in handwritten work. This belief makes life difficult for many children and is pretty outdated.[2]

It saddens me when I hear that learners have resisted using a supportive aid - for example, a laptop, voice recorder, tabletop aid, pastel-coloured paper - because they don't want to feel "different" or "singled out". In a truly inclusive school, all ways of working would be actively promoted and encouraged, and the benefits of this will be experienced by *all* members of the school community.

IDEAS FOR PROMOTING DYSLEXIA-FRIENDLY CULTURE

1. Remember, dyslexia impacts the whole curriculum; think of it as everyone's business.

Voices of Dyslexia

> *"The biggest thing that worked for us as a school was when the subject leaders were asked to include a dyslexia slot in all their staff meeting presentations – this showed that practice was working across the curriculum."*
>
> Gill, SENCO

2. Involve everyone. Talk to your support staff, your PPA cover teachers, your visitors, your parents. Whether it's the small group of angry parents on the playground, or the resistant teacher who has always done things the same way, a minority of resistance can be deeply held; collaboration can change this.
3. Look beyond achievement and learning in the classroom to the whole experience of the dyslexic learner in school.
4. Find ways to share existing practice with other staff members, other schools and parents.

Voices of Dyslexia

> *"The other amazing thing is that Oliver won an award at school for progress in handwriting. And it was actually something that lots of schools took part in and he actually got to go up on stage and collect a medal and a certificate. It was amazing as his parents to see that because, again, that was all down to his perseverance, that he'd come that far."*
>
> Pippa, parent[3]

5. Celebrate diversity. There is so much to celebrate about children with dyslexia. It's a myth that all dyslexics have the same strengths, and it would be a disservice to your learners to assume this in school. However, there are many commonalities. Many children with dyslexia are creative. Many have a good imagination, are good communicators and work well with patterns. Many are resilient (they've had to be) and intuitive. Dyslexia occurs across the ability range; some are extremely clever while some struggle in many areas, but *all* children with dyslexia have relative strengths. Sadly, these are not always easy to find in earlier schooling, but it's essential that we do.

Voices of Dyslexia

> *"I would say my experience of having a child with dyslexia has mainly been positive, I think because the school has done such a great job of making everyone equal and really debunking the myths around dyslexia, meaning that you're stupid or that you're behind. It's the fact that you process information differently. It's helped that in school they had a specific assembly where they talked about famous faces who were dyslexic. So this is another step forward that really makes it more mainstream and less taboo, something to be ashamed about, which it really isn't. It's great that we're finding ways to educate people better so that we all feel more positive and supportive going forward."*
>
> Lisa Barclay[4]

7. Value individual strengths rather than stereotypical labels. It can sometimes be unhelpful to create stereotypes around dyslexia. I recently laughed when I received an email from someone that she gets tired of hearing constantly about

Richard Branson as a typical dyslexic. Not all dyslexics will establish a world-wide empire (but a few will)! What is most important for inclusive culture is to value all strengths, abilities and achievements.

> *"In an ideal world we would understand what a child needs. We would value what they bring, and their strengths. We'd help them to understand what they find difficult or tricky and work out what works for them. We'd empower them to find ways which work for them."*
>
> Gill, SENCO[5]

8. Be mindful of your language and interactions. "Ableist language" refers to words, phrases or expressions that discriminate against or marginalise people with disabilities. Some types of ableist language can be harder to detect by those who do not have a disability, and this is particularly pertinent in relation to dyslexia, which can be more "hidden" than some disabilities and difficulties. As you read the examples below, reflect on the underlying message for a child with dyslexia.

   "If you can't listen properly, you'll have to stay in at break and do it then."

   Children with working memory difficulties hear that they will lose their needed break because of something they can't control.

   "We're now going to write up our work neatly so it can go on display."

   Children hear that their writing is only worthy of celebration in a neat form and that work in progress is less valid than a finished product.

   "I'm going to give a reward for the child who can read the most books over the summer."

Children hear that quantity matters more than quality. Slow and hesitant readers feel their efforts are less valuable.

"Well done to all those who have finished all their work. You have worked really hard!"

Children with slow processing speed hear that they are not working as hard as those who can work more quickly.

"You've had five minutes to write the date and learning objective. You should have finished it by now!"

Children with slow processing speed, working memory difficulties and writing difficulties hear that copying quickly is an important skills, and that their effort is not good enough.

This type of unhelpful language needs to be named and rooted out, whether by examining yourself or examining your colleagues. Listening carefully to the language we use from the perspective of a child with dyslexia can be incredibly informative!

9. Listen, then listen, and listen again.

"In teachers, open mindedness, understanding and tolerance was really the most important thing. Any teachers that were not interested in making exceptions for my strategies didn't help at all, put me in a difficult spot and made things harder for me. But the teachers that were understanding, and understood that I had strategies, and let me use them, those were the most helpful teachers."

Fred, now adult[6]

Active listening can be transformational. In my experience, educators who reflect on their interaction with learners are always the most inclusive. Listening needs to be intentional, because interactions in our busy and pressurised school life are all too often focused on procedure, behaviour and lesson content.

10. Prepare your learners for the future. It's alarmingly easy for teachers to forget that our ultimate goal is preparing children for the future. This is a future which embraces a wide range of skills, abilities and intelligences, and it's tragic that our underfunded schools are not as able to reflect the changing world as much as they would like. School culture needs to be challenged by this changing world, where spelling is increasingly unimportant, and technology, creativity and different thinking skills are taking centre stage. There is a lot that children with dyslexia can teach us!
11. Review continually. Inclusion is a process. As such, it is an unending quest to find better ways of responding to diversity. I see a large number of schools that promote dyslexia-friendly practice and seek to change culture. However, I see fewer schools that are dedicated to constantly reviewing their practice to evaluate what's working and what needs changing. It's worth dedicating regular time to gather information and ask questions. Here are some examples:
    - As staff and children come and go, is there still a common understanding of inclusive learning in your class/phase/school? Are the strategies you use still relevant?
    - What has changed in recent years? This could be with your school staff, learners or external factors such as policy and curriculum. How does this impact your inclusive practice?
    - What data are you gathering? Is this reflective of learning preferences? Is the emphasis too heavily on written skills? Are you listening to pupil voice and consulting with community stakeholders?
    - Are children actively encouraged to innovate and try things out?
    - Are you learning from and building on mistakes? And encouraging learners to do the same?
    - Do teachers and support staff have opportunities to observe and learn from each other and share good practice?

- Do you share your resources and ideas with other staff?
- Do you actively listen to your learners?

QUICK WINS

Here are some easy, prep-free ideas for developing a dyslexia-friendly culture that you can do straight away.

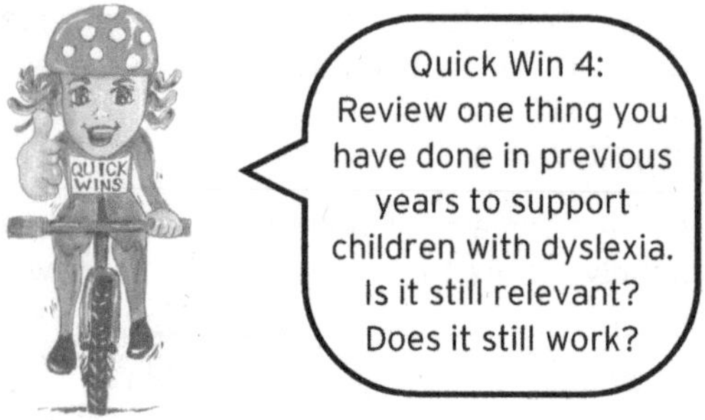

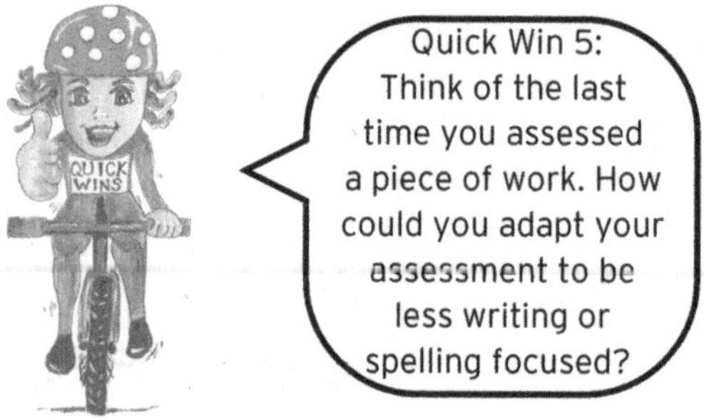

NOTES

1 Hall, E. (1976). *Beyond Culture*. New York: Knopf Publishing Group.
2 Sobel, D. and Alston, S. (2021). The Inclusive Classroom. London: Bloomsbury Education, p.98.
3 Pippa's story on film can be found on the Voices of Dyslexia project page, https://louiseselbydyslexia.com/voices-of-dyslexia-do-you-have-a-story-to-tell
4 Lisa's story on film can be found on the Voices of Dyslexia project page, https://louiseselbydyslexia.com/voices-of-dyslexia-do-you-have-a-story-to-tell
5 Gill's story on film can be found on the Voices of Dyslexia project page, https://louiseselbydyslexia.com/voices-of-dyslexia-do-you-have-a-story-to-tell
6 Fred's story can be found on film on the Voices of Dyslexia Project page, https://louiseselbydyslexia.com/voices-of-dyslexia-do-you-have-a-story-to-tell

11

THE DYSLEXIA-FRIENDLY LEARNING ENVIRONMENT

In Chapter 10, we discussed the learning culture, which is all about embedded practices and beliefs – those customs that are embedded in the whole identity of a school. In this chapter, we explore the practical outworking of this, which is the learning environment. Environmental factors can play an important role in creating, or reducing, barriers that compromise a learner's experience at school.[1] This includes all learners. Environment embraces more than just displays and classrooms; it is the space and surroundings in which learners are supported, led and nurtured in their learning. In this chapter, we'll consider four aspects of the learning environment: physical space, virtual space, celebrating diversity and resources. All the photographs in this chapter have been provided by the two schools featured in the case studies in "Hearing from the experts", St Joseph and St Bede RC Primary School, Bury, and Zouch Academy and Nursery, Tidworth.

TIPS TOP TIPS

Before we dig deeper, here are some top tips for developing a dyslexia-friendly learning environment.

1. Start with the child. Think: what would help you?
2. Use your display to relieve cognitive load.
3. Utilise your learners' strengths.

DOI: 10.4324/9781003401544-14

4. Create a multi-sensory environment.
5. Ensure consistency.
6. Check accessibility.
7. Back up auditory information.
8. Be clear about purpose.
9. Be flexible and adaptable.
10. Commit time to teaching learners know to use displays, learning aids and resources.

1. PHYSICAL SPACE

CLASSROOMS

Ensure classrooms are well lit and there is adequate space for learners to write and read in comfort. Check height of tables and chairs.

SEATING

- Left-handers need space to their left; avoid seating them with right-handers immediately to their left.
- Seat learners with dyslexia close to the front with clear visibility of the board. This helps minimise distraction and reduce copying difficulties.
- Seat dyslexic learners within the teacher's peripheral vision so they, and the teacher, can pick up on non-verbal communication.

DISPLAY

> For many children, when it comes to display, less is more. If we wish them to focus on learning, we need to avoid filling the classroom with unnecessary distraction that make it harder for them to concentrate. We need to focus on making the environment as supportive as possible, balancing the competing demands of stimulation, support for focus and prompts for learning. There is no magic

> formula for this, and the balance will vary from class to class and room to room.[2]

When I started teaching in the late 1990s, the emphasis was on presentation and decoration. I remember spending hours at the weekend creating beautiful displays of children's work. Of course, display needs to look attractive and appealing, but I'm so glad to have seen the change over the years from a culture where "everything is perfect and looks beautiful" to a culture where our environment informs and supports children's learning. For children with literacy difficulties, this is paramount. There must be a celebration of work in progress, work that might look untidy but is nevertheless considered excellent, and work presented in different formats.

General tips for display:

- Check visibility, especially key words/spellings and information regularly needed – round the corner beside the toilets is no use when you are sitting at your desk!
- Include handwriting as well as typeface, in display – but ensure it is consistent with your school policy.
- As well as informing learning and celebrating success, ensure that your displays demonstrate work in progress.

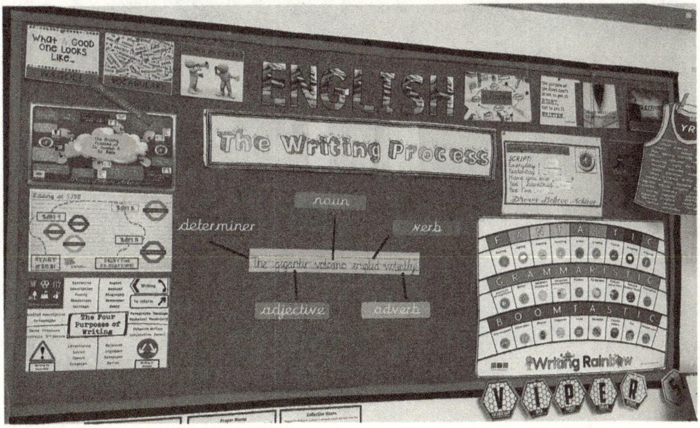

FIGURE 11.1 Display work in progress

- Display planning and editing as well as finished products, and show examples of note taking and study skills (e.g. highlighting, mind-mapping, bullet points).
- Display a variety of methods of recording (e.g. sound bites, images, concrete materials, mind-maps).
- Display visual timetables – this is always good practice for everyone! Just make sure they are age-appropriate and visible.
- Task plans and regular self-monitoring checklists can be useful to display on walls and/or tables.
- Display spellings that are used regularly, ideally on tabletop aids as well as walls. This includes the "little" common words that are often tricky for learners with dyslexia. For example:
  - Days and months, seasons.
  - Alphabet (lower and upper case). Some learners throughout the primary phases struggle with alphabetical order, letter names and letter formation as well. The alphabet should be displayed in every class on the wall and/or tabletops, and this can be done in an age-appropriate way.

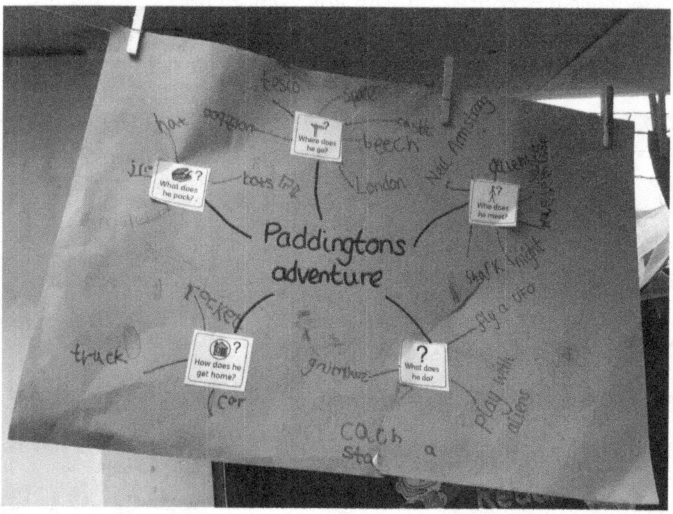

FIGURE 11.2 Display work in progress

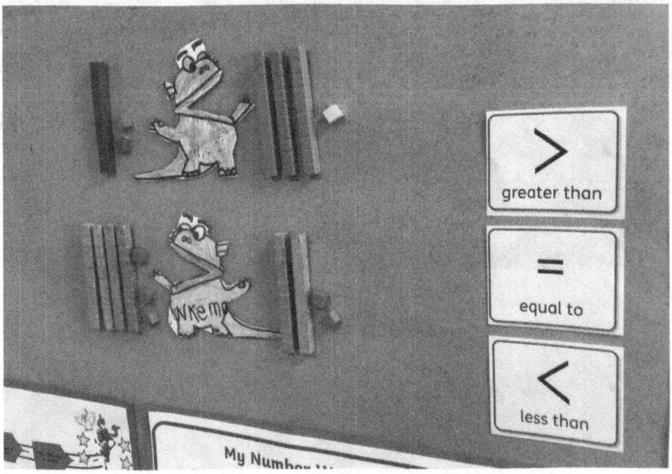

FIGURE 11.3 Display different methods of recording

    ○ Key words (including high-frequency words). Remember that dyslexic learners across the age span may be able to spell topic words, but may still struggle with common high-frequency words such as for, said, their.

- Vocabulary and regularly used topic words.
- Display number lines clearly – these can be age-appropriate (e.g. negative numbers and 100 squares for older learners) but ensure the sequence is in steps of 1 to support difficulties with counting on and back.
- Display language of maths. Colour coding can support memory (but make this consistent across the school).

LABELLING RESOURCES

Ensure all resources for children to use are clearly labelled. Use pictures as well as words for your labels, even in upper primary school, in order to relieve unnecessary load.

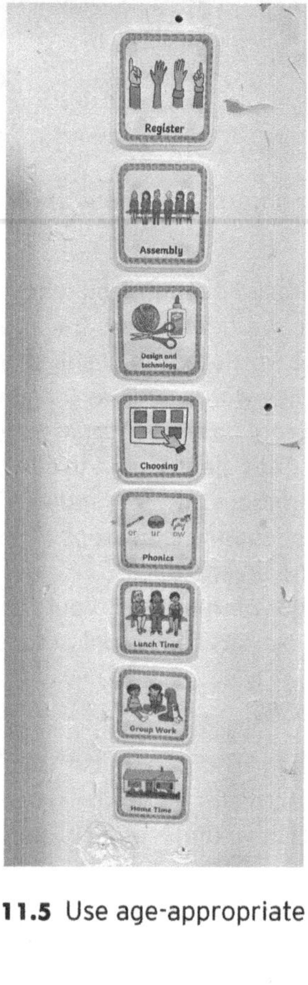

FIGURES 11.4 AND 11.5 Use age-appropriate visual timetables

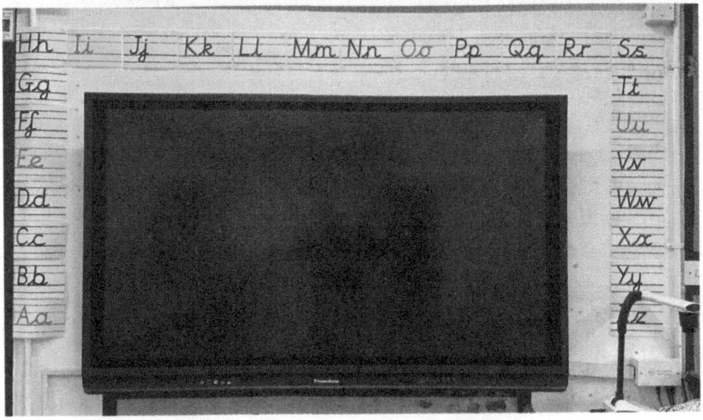

FIGURES 11.6 AND 11.7 Display the alphabet

BACKGROUND COLOURS AND MOVING TEXT

- Avoid black text on white; the colour of the paper or screen is less important (unless a qualified optometrist has recommended specific accommodations).
- If laminating for wall display, use matt pouches for display to avoid glare.

FIGURE 11.8 Display vocabulary

- Set the whiteboard screen to an off-white background - grey, cream or a pastel colour - and follow suit with computers and devices.

FONTS AND TEXT ON DISPLAY

- Look for fonts which are clear and easy for all children to read. Beware of fonts which claim to be "dyslexia-friendly"; sometimes these are more designed for those children with visual difficulties, and can be difficult for other children to read. Look for a font that is sans serif and uncomplicated, with well-rounded and spaced-out letters. Examples are:

Arial	Comic Sans	Quicksand	Verdana	Tahoma
Century Gothic	Trebuchet	Calibri	Chalkboard	Sassoon
Imprima	Futura	Open Sans	Cadman	

FIGURE 11.9 Label resources with words and pictures

- Ensure spacing between words is adequate so that words can be clearly distinguished.
- Avoid underlining and italics, as this can cause crowding, and use bold, highlighting or different colours for emphasis.
- In display, avoid using all upper-case letters for continuous text. Lower-case letters, or capitalised titles, are easier to read.
- When displaying handwriting, adhere to the school handwriting policy.

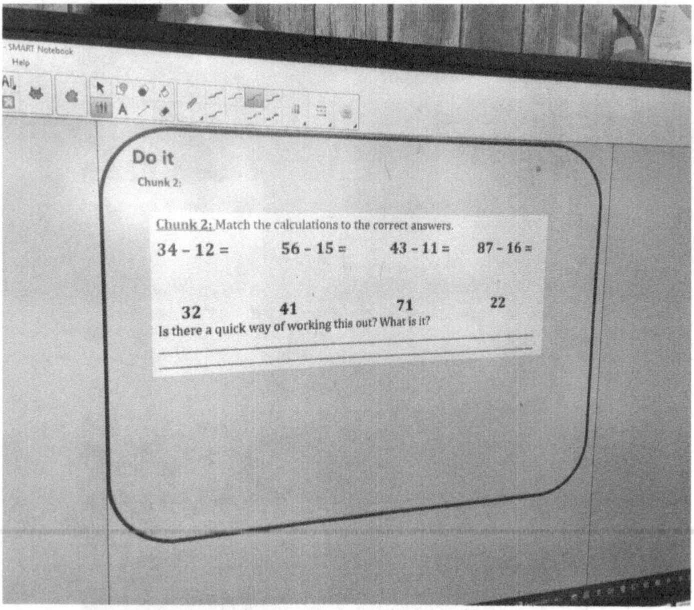

FIGURE 11.10 Set whiteboard screen to off-white

2. VIRTUAL SPACE

WEBSITE

Websites which are dyslexia-friendly:

- use clear, legible font (see above)
- offer text-to-speech facilities
- avoid black on white
- present text clearly and well spaced out
- use a variety of media (e.g. graphics, video and audio files)
- offer accessibility features such as text-to-speech, reading mask, reading guide, text magnifier, visually pleasing experience (e.g. enlarge text), background colour adjustment, highlight titles, highlight links, increase letter spacing, increase line height, big cursor. Examples of these can be found on www.louiseselbydyslexia.com by scrolling down to the bottom on the home page in the "Accessibility tools" section.

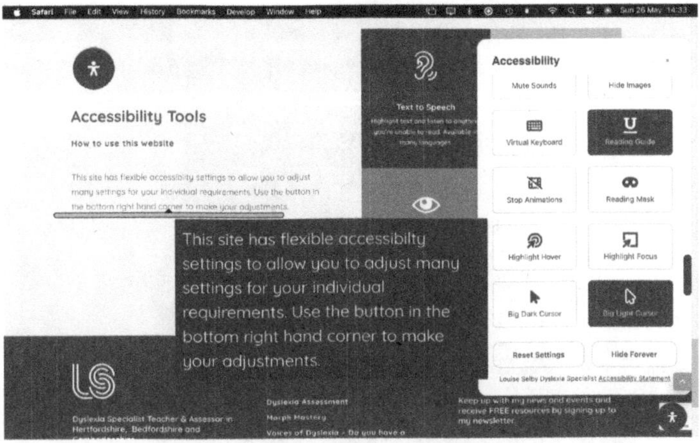

FIGURE 11.11 Provide accessibility features on website

FIGURE 11.12 QR codes enable independent access to learning platform

FIGURES 11.13, 11.14 AND 11.15 Class help stations enable children to go and find the resource they need

FIGURES 11.13, 11.14 AND 11.15 Continued

- Learning platform
- If you're lucky enough to have an online learning platform, many of the above points about websites apply here too. The learning platform is a great opportunity to provide:
- films or audio files of instructions/procedures/task lists that can easily be forgotten (e.g. how to do the grid method in multiplication)
- visual aids/learning support
- examples of finished versions
- feedback/marking that is not pen and paper based.

The learning platform also enhances independence, as learners may upload their work themselves and can be independent in recording, filming and using apps. Figure 11.12 is an example of how one school uses QR codes to enable easy access for children.

3. CELEBRATING DIVERSITY: "I DO IT DIFFERENTLY"

The learning environment can reflect values and support positive identity by reflecting diversity.

Use the environment to positively reflect different ways of working. For example:

- Include books and publications about dyslexia and neurodiversity.
- Include "higher level lower interest books" in your class displays and selections.
- Display learning aids not just as a way of supporting learning but to celebrate the way we learn and encourage metacognition.
- "This is how I learn" displays highlight the different strategies used by different learners.
- "Thinking" displays reflect how children went through the process of learning.

3. RESOURCES

Use your environment to provide accessible resources that reduce unnecessary barriers to learning. For example:

- Provide help sheets, word banks and handouts for anything that is written on the board.

Voices of Dyslexia

"Trying to write and spell words was a hurdle for me and as a result I often fell behind having to look at the blackboard more frequently while trying to copy into my jotter what the teacher would write. I often struggled to keep up with what we had to copy. Often the teachers would flick around the blackboard and I was unable to keep up."

Elaine, now adult

- Readily available resources for taking notes include sticky notes and labels, highlighter pens, note pads and mini-whiteboards.
- Concrete and multi-sensory resources for literacy and maths should be available in all stages of primary school. These could be provided as individual learning packs, tabletop resource banks or class help stations, where children can independently go and find the resource they need.
- Tactile letters and small whiteboards can be ideal for learners to "have a go" at spellings.
- Have a range of writing instruments and pencil/pen grips readily available in every class, including pens and pencils suitable for left-handers.
- Provide desktop re-usable phoneme frames, b/d cue cards, alphabet strips, word banks with days and months, key words.
- Have task lists and plans for individual tasks, or generic (e.g. editing check lists), and prompt sheets.
- Provide reading rulers (to support with tracking text) and coloured overlays for children to try.
- Use symbols/pictures to support written text wherever possible.
- Pastel-coloured exercise books and paper for children with visual difficulties are generally available at a reasonable price from county supplies; these can be helpful for some children. Specialist paper can also be used.
- Ensure that dictionaries are at appropriate stages.

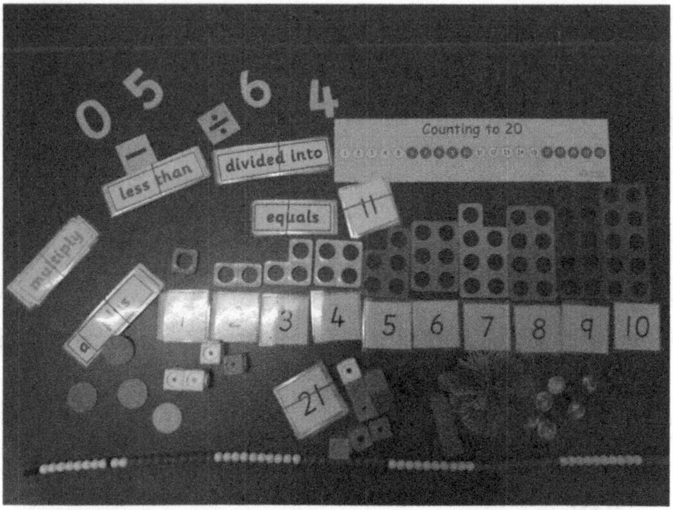

FIGURES 11.16 AND 11.17 Concrete and multi-sensory resources

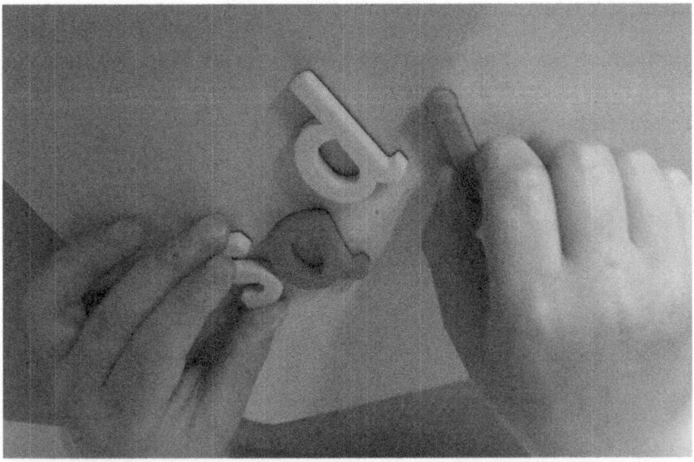

FIGURES 11.18 AND 11.19 Tactile letters help learners "have a go" at spellings.

QUICK WINS

We'll finish this chapter with some easy, prep-free ideas for creating a dyslexia-friendly learning environment that you can do straight away.

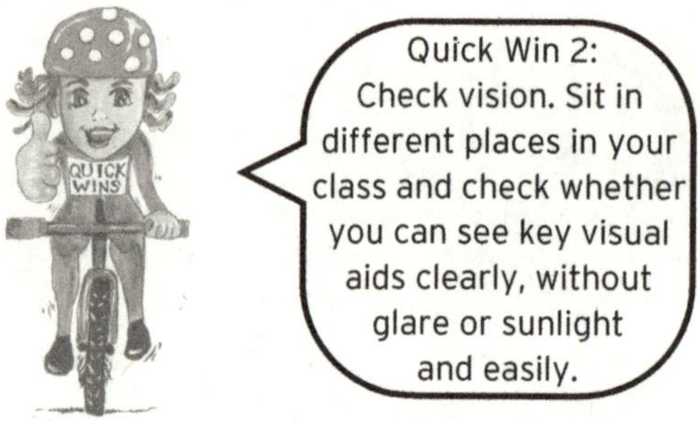

NOTES

1 Education Endowment Foundation (2021). Special Educational Needs in Mainstream School Guidance Report, https://educationendowmentfoundation.org.uk/education-evidence/guidance-reports/send

2 Sobel, D. & Alston, S, (2021). *The Inclusive Classroom*. London: Bloomsbury Education, p.43.

12

INTERVENTION

TOP TIPS

Before we dig deeper, here are some top tips for planning intervention for learners with dyslexia

1. Ensure someone is overseeing, monitoring and evaluating intervention.
2. Ensure adults delivering intervention are equipped with sufficient time and resources.
3. Plan and evaluate for impact.
4. Be clear about what you are targeting.
5. Allocate time for communication.
6. Manage expectations of impact.
7. Make sure it's happening!

Most dyslexics need targeted intervention at some point in their schooling. The more I talk to children with literacy difficulties about what has worked for them, the more I realise that targeted intervention is directly linked with independence and resilience in class learning, because of the huge impact of intervention on motivation and confidence. Motivation has a direct impact on self-regulation and metacognition in class.

Lindsay's description of the impact of intervention beyond the data is powerful.

DOI: 10.4324/9781003401544-15

"Moving through to secondary school, my daughter had some interventions in spelling and reading, which were really, really useful for her moving forward. And now she's in high school and absolutely thriving. She walks back in through the door every day, just excited and thrilled by the things that she's learning and the work that she's doing, she gets a lot of praise for her homework, what she does on the computer."

Lindsay, parent[1]

In an age of slashed school budgets, it's more essential than ever that intervention offers value for money, and this requires planning and evaluation. Intervention needs to show impact against what it is targeted for. Over the years, I have worked with a number of schools on evaluating impact against cost and developing strategy for making the most of (very limited) budgets. I have observed some common pitfalls in planning intervention. Below are some guiding principles that I have drawn from my experience of effective intervention and discussion with others.

"Some specific dyslexia training really helped me to understand what individual learners need. I felt more equipped. As a SENCO, knowing how interventions worked and understanding them was vital, so I knew how they should be delivered."

Gill, SENCO

1. Be clear about what the need is that you are addressing and evaluate whether the intervention can meet this need. "Dyslexia intervention" is not enough - break down the dyslexia into the area(s) of need, such as spelling, phonics, reading, comprehension, accessing learning, accessing lessons, consolidating learning, sentence writing, etc.
2. Ensure the person delivering the intervention has the required expertise.

> The practitioner is the intervention. We need to ensure that staff have the support, expertise, knowledge, and agency to support their learners. Consistent, high quality staff are critically important.[2]

3. Allocate time for planning and communications. Include this in your evaluation of whether an intervention is manageable. Interventions requiring planning time do not work if planning time is not allocated.
4. Ensure someone qualified (usually the class teacher or SENCO) is overseeing and evaluating the intervention.
5. Ensure the pace is appropriate; remember some dyslexics have slower processing speed and require multiple opportunities for over-learning.
6. Multi-sensory is best. This can be using tactile equipment (e.g. letters, cards, spinners), talking, touch screens, movement, visuals, pictures, video, etc.
7. Communicate with parents so that they can support at home.
8. Timetable it! It won't happen otherwise! Keep a register (Figure 12.1). Ideally, this can show not just whether sessions

1:1 Intervention Register

Name of intervention: **Pupil's name:** **Date:** **Number of sessions allocated per week:**

Week number & date	Monday	Tuesday	Wednesday	Thursday	Friday
Comments from TA:			Comments from teacher:		
Comments from TA:			Comments from teacher:		
Comments from TA:			Comments from teacher:		
Comments from TA:			Comments from teacher:		
Comments from TA:			Comments from teacher:		
√ = session took place		C = child absent or unavailable		A = adult absent or unavailable	

LOUISE SELBY Intervention Register

FIGURE 12.1 Intervention register

take place, but if they didn't, why they didn't. It's often because the adult is unavailable, sometimes being asked to do three things at the same time! This type of register helps with monitoring impact too. So often interventions fail not because of the methodology, but because they are in fact hardly ever taking place!

9. Measure impact to ensure that you are providing value for money - even the cheapest interventions need to be evaluated for impact. Impact data does not need to be assessment data alone. It can measured in a range of qualitative ways - for example, pupil and parent interviews, work scrutiny, observation.
10. Manage expectations when evaluating data. Remember that dyslexia is a persistent, significant difficulty with specific areas of learning. Some (but not all) learners with dyslexia will make very slow, small steps of progress, and may not "catch up" in the way you expect from booster-type interventions for children who need a little extra support.

TYPES OF INTERVENTION

There are so many interventions available that it can be difficult to know which to choose. Not all learners with dyslexia need the same intervention at the same time. Below is an outline of different types of interventions, with pros and cons, to help you decide. This is illustrated in Table 12.1, which is also available as a colour PDF for download by following the access instructions at the start of this book.

TABLE 12.1 School-based intervention for dyslexia

Intervention	*Used for*	*Pros*	*Cons*
Personalised intervention to target gaps and/or underlying skills	Supporting learners with persistent and significant difficulties with a specific area of learning, e.g. word reading, phonics, spelling, reading comprehension, writing	Meets actual, rather than perceived, needs Allows for structure, over-learning, multi-sensory teaching and learner to work at his/her own pace Assessment informed Usually works where other interventions fail	Time-consuming: usually needs prep time as well as contact time Not usually directly linked to what's happening in the classroom – focuses more on underlying skills Requires some training
Individual reading support	Practice to support fluency and over-learning	No preparation involved Can be "little and often" Easily timetabled and learner does not miss much lesson time	Does not teach underlying and specific reading skills and knowledge e.g. phonic decoding, phonological awareness, morphology

Intervention	*Used for*	*Pros*	*Cons*
Computer-based intervention programmes	Supporting reading and/or spelling, usually word level skills and knowledge	Does not use much, if any, adult time, minimal preparation Some have an assessment which defines entry level and measures progress	Not usually personalised; may not address gaps Not as multi-sensory as other approaches Can move too fast and not provide enough over-learning opportunities
Precision teaching	Over-learning something that has been taught	"Little and often", less lesson time missed Supports over-learning and fluency Targets specific gaps and is personalised	Does not "teach", just enables practice, dyslexics may need content to be taught first Generally not multi-sensory Can be dull

(*Continued*)

TABLE 12.1 (Continued)

Intervention	*Used for*	*Pros*	*Cons*
Pre-teaching (1:1 or group)	Enabling learners to access lessons by preparing them for text, vocabulary that will be taught, etc.	Learners are more likely to access lessons without needing support or catch up Reduces barriers to learning for dyslexic (e.g. working memory, slower processing, reading difficulties)	Needs to be delivered by teacher, or if a different adult is delivering, they need prep time or time with teacher in advance Does not address specific gaps, not assessment led
Consolidation work (1:1 or group)	Enabling learners to consolidate learning by e.g. re-reading, explaining, discussing	Provides over-learning that many dyslexics need Not labour-intensive Can address misunderstandings immediately	Does not address individual needs May not offer enough over-learning for those with significant, persistent difficulties

Intervention	*Used for*	*Pros*	*Cons*
Guided/group work e.g. reading	Targeting specific skills linked to whole-class learning, e.g. guided reading, guided writing	Can support groups of learners with common difficulties Linked to class work More children are supported at one time, therefore cost-effective	Does not address individual needs May not offer enough over-learning for those with significant, persistent difficulties
Learning skills support	Supports learning to organise learning, memory skills, use of assistive technology	Supports metacognition (learning how to learn) Enhances independence and autonomy Teaches transferable skills	Does not teach specific skills required within curriculum subjects Does not address gaps, not assessment led

QUICK WINS

Here are some easy, prep-free ideas for planning intervention that you can do straight away.

NOTES

1 Lindsay's story on film can be found on the Voices of Dyslexia project page, https://louiseselbydyslexia.com/voices-of-dyslexia-do-you-have-a-story-to-tell
2 Potter, C. and Rowland, M. (2024). Pupil premium and SEND: learning without labels. Unity Research School, https://researchschool.org.uk/unity/news/pupil-premium-and-send-learning-without-labels

13

TRANSITION

Transition can be a frightening time for children with dyslexia (and, indeed, all children). There's fear of learning being even more challenging, fear of not being able to access support, of reading difficulties being exposed, of not keeping up. Children worry about increased sanctions for not finishing work, or not staying on task, and they anticipate being taught by unsympathetic adults. Some children fear tests and assessments, some worry about academic grouping, some wonder how they will organise themselves with new routines and fear their difficulties with this will get them into trouble. This chapter offers some tips to support transition across the different phases of education.

TOP TIPS

Before we dig deeper, here are some top tips for transition planning for learners with dyslexia

1. Prioritise communication, and include children and parents in this.
2. Be aware of different learning challenges at different stages.
3. Use pupil passports - involve the child and parents, and focus on needs rather than diagnosis.
4. Consider fatigue.
5. Ensure children know that teachers talk to each other!

DOI: 10.4324/9781003401544-16

TRANSITION INTO NEW CLASSES

Early communication is always helpful. It may seem obvious, but children don't always know that teachers talk to each other! Individual conversations with children who have additional support strategies is a really effective way to ease children's concerns. Remember to ask the child what works and check it still works. Sometimes children's needs change, so transition into a new class is a great opportunity to review them! Children will benefit from reassurance about the level of the work expected from them in the new year group; many will anticipate that they will all of a sudden be expected to work at a much higher level than they have been.

TRANSITION FROM EARLY YEARS FOUNDATION STAGE (AGE 3–5) INTO KEY STAGE 1 (AGE 5–7)

At this point, a child with dyslexia has probably been identified as delayed in reading and writing, and may present with attention difficulties. They will also be experiencing more than usual fatigue. Often this transition is a tricky jump for these children. In Year 1, learning can become much more formal, with more requirement to sit at tables and write, less child-initiated learning and fewer opportunities to learn through play. It's really important that this transition is eased for them; continued opportunities to learn informally will be vital.

TRANSITION FROM KEY STAGE 1 (AGE 5–7) INTO KEY STAGE 2 (AGE 7–11)

It's often around age 7 when parents report that they first have concerns about their child's development. By this time, children are usually all too aware of how hard they are finding learning, and the focus on reading and writing can be gruelling. At this age, fatigue and frustration can be overwhelming for children and parents. For teachers to understand that children with dyslexia and specific learning difficulties are often exhausted at the end of lessons is helpful, and discussing with parents how to accommodate increasing demands on homework can also ease transition and help with home life too! It will be important to establish a strong focus on supporting self-esteem and establishing learners' strengths and talents. This is also often a time when comprehension difficulties begin to emerge, as children who have been taught to decode well may still lack fluency, and reading can still be very effortful. Support with comprehension across the curriculum and providing time and opportunity for consolidation and pre-teaching may be significant factors in effective transition.

TRANSITION FROM KEY STAGE 2 (AGE 7–11) INTO KEY STAGE 3 (AGE 11–14)

Voices of Dyslexia

"I have found the transition from primary to secondary a very different experience, and it became clear very quickly that none of my daughter's teachers knew she had dyslexia."

Julie, parent

The radical change in teaching styles from one class teacher to individual subject teachers can be exciting, but overwhelming. There are also, obviously, a lot more teachers involved with the child, and communicating needs with all the these is challenging for the SENCO! Learners with dyslexia may struggle with a number of challenges during this transition:

- fatigue and overwhelm
- organising their belongings, finding their way around, losing equipment
- keeping up with the increased pace of learning
- secondary teachers across the curriculum in general having less understanding of reading difficulties
- fewer teaching assistants to support in lessons
- the increased stigma of reading and writing difficulties and fear of being "singled out" for intervention
- fear of being asked to read aloud in class
- the logistics of communication when the learner has many teachers; are all teachers aware?
- anxiety about tests and academic groupings

- increase in frequency of tests and requirement to "revise"
- increased need to use online learning systems and computers

Additional transition days, where the child can ask questions and see some Year 7 lessons, are really helpful. Communication between teachers, SENCOs and with the child and parents is also useful. On entering secondary school, primary children come with different experience of technology. It's useful for primary teachers to find out what is on offer for their dyslexic learners once they know which school they are going to, and support them with learning how to use these.

"We had touch typing that was put in place which has been absolutely invaluable. So before my daughter left primary school, she could touch type fluently, which has been an absolute godsend for her."

Lindsay, parent[1]

PUPIL PASSPORTS

A pupil passport, also sometimes known as a "one-page profile" or "pen portrait" is a single-page resource created by the teacher or SENCO in discussion with parents and the child. It is extremely useful at times of transition. It outlines a learner's key strengths and needs, and the main strategies and adaptations that are needed across the curriculum. Pupil passports should always involve the learner, and the learner should always agree with the final product and any reviews. It serves as an accessible way of presenting information to all teachers and adults involved with the learner, and it always includes a photo of the learner, so that new and supply staff can use the strategies straight away. The passport is a working document, and best practice is that it is frequently discussed, reviewed and updated. As learners get older, they should be encouraged to take responsibility themselves for updating pupil passports.

Figure 13.1 (also available as online Support Material for download) shows a pupil passport example that works well for a

Date: January 2024

Sample Pupil Passport for Primary Age (dyslexia)

My strengths and qualities

I am creative, imaginative and come up with some great ideas, especially for drama and history work. I make great films! I am kind and understanding.

How I learn

I have dyslexia. I understand well but I have difficulty with working quickly, holding information in my head while working on it and reading and spelling. I have plenty of great ideas but sometimes struggle to write them down, and sometimes I need help with this. I need to see as well as hear and having pictures or videos of what I am going to do helps me. I learn best when I can use computers, and I love making films, presentations and podcasts, and I love being creative.

How best to support me

Please give me instructions in steps, preferably with pictures, and write them down.

Please help me to remember what you say by giving me images or films to help, and giving me the information in chunks. It helps if I get to do something between each chunk.

Let me record my ideas in different ways (like posters, flow charts, podcasts, powerpoint), and let me use computers.

Give me enough time, don't rush me, and let me have brain breaks. Please understand that I can work well, but not quickly.

Give me spellings I'll need, and don't focus too much on spelling when you give me feedback.

Literacy based activities

Give me word banks that provide spellings I need for a piece of work. I like to plan these myself.

Help me to read texts in advance of lessons.

Give me writing frames to help me get my ideas down.

Let me use dictation software for some writing tasks, and let me use computer readers for difficult texts.

Maths based activities

Help me with oral/mental work - I might need to make notes or have visual aids.

Help me to do my learning in steps; I find it hard to hold a lot of maths in my head if I need to work with it as well.

Give me number fact sheets to help when I'm calculating, as I forget these easily.

Resources

Computers and read aloud/dictate facilities, word banks, writing frames, visual aids for number facts

Please avoid

Asking me to read out loud.

Asking me to work too quickly (I am pretty good at knowing what I can do) or giving me sanctions for not finishing.

Asking me to stay in at play time - I really need my breaks.

Giving me long messages to remember.

FIGURE 13.1 Pupil passport example for a child with dyslexia child with dyslexia. Essentially, it should include a recent photo, strengths and qualities, comments about how the child learns, how best to support the learner, strategies that work (include across the curriculum as well), resources and what to avoid. The profile should reflect the child's views throughout, so a separate section about the child's views is not necessary. The focus should be on needs, not diagnosis; focus on what teachers can do to support. Ideally, use font and colours that the child has chosen or agreed.

WORKING WITH PARENTS

Parents have a key role in supporting transition. Keep them informed and involved as much as you can. Parents are most likely to know what their child is worrying about, which may be very different to what you expect! Some things parents can do to support transition are:

- Find out some topics that are covered in the next year. Explore fun ways to learn about these topics (e.g. museums, activity days, TV programmes).
- Support the child with learning to use assistive technology (e.g. spellcheck, read aloud, dictate, immersive reader). There are free workshops available online to support this (see "Further resources" section).
- Enable the child to learn to touch type.

For secondary transition (in addition to the above):

- Prepare the child for the journey and, if possible, practise it together.
- Support the child with what to get organised for the day and set up some organisation systems (e.g. a folder for letters, box for school books). Set up a routine and stick to it.
- Keep a family calendar updated and encourage your child to use it too.

- Before the end of term, ensure you know how to communicate with the school and who should be your first port of call (usually the form tutor).
- Keep a physical record of web addresses, logins and passwords for all learning platforms your child is expected to use.

QUICK WINS

Here are some easy, prep-free ideas for planning transition that you can do straight away.

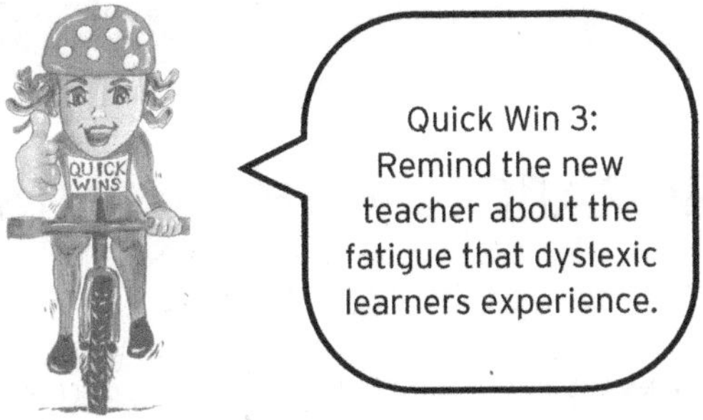

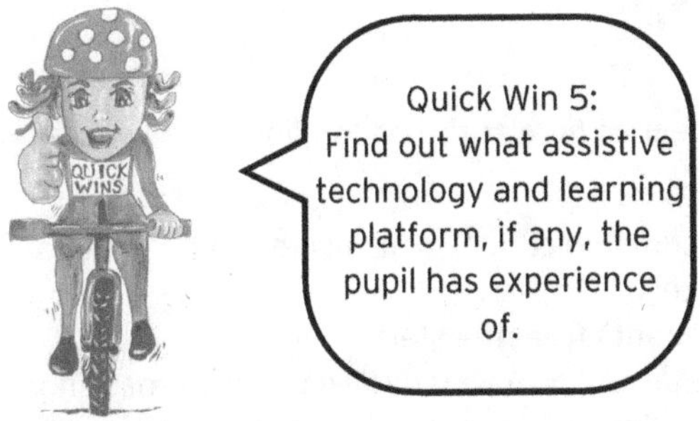

NOTE

1 Lindsay's story on film can be found on the Voices of Dyslexia project page, https://louiseselbydyslexia.com/voices-of-dyslexia-do-you-have-a-story-to-tell

14

COLLABORATION WITH PARENTS

This chapter discusses the importance of working with parents. It considers the value of listening and offers some strategies to enable cooperative relationships with parents. It also discusses the balance between managing expectations of parents who are very demanding and working productively with them.

Parents bring in-depth knowledge of their child's strengths, weaknesses and learning preferences, while schools offer expertise in educational strategies and resources. In an ideal world, this is a perfect match! In this chapter, we'll explore some strategies to achieve good collaborative relationships with parents.

TOP TIPS

Before we dig deeper, here are some top tips for collaboration with parents

1. Prioritise communication, and include children and parents in this.
2. Listen to parents from the start.
3. Be aware that children with dyslexia may be masking their difficulties, and parents may know a different story to teachers.
4. Aim to pre-empt parental concern by communicating positively from the start.
5. Keep parents informed about reputable dyslexia organisations and support groups.

DOI: 10.4324/9781003401544-17

6. Remember parents may have literacy difficulties themselves.
7. Be prepared to work with parents in working out what works.

WHEN COLLABORATION WORKS

Voices of Dyslexia

"We've been lucky that school have been very supportive. He's had lots of extra practice out of the classroom for his reading, for his phonics, for his handwriting. And for us it's just a major celebration in our house now that he can read independently. He's just taking those first baby steps."

Pippa, parent[1]

Regular communication between parents and school encourages a culture of flexibility and openness to review. It means that potential issues are identified early on. Collaboration also helps to foster a supportive and inclusive environment, where the child feels understood, valued and empowered to overcome challenges associated with dyslexia.

In an ideal world, we would not need to have a diagnosis of dyslexia at all, as all needs would be met, which was Carole's experience for most of primary school:

Voices of Dyslexia

"The school were supportive so we saw no need to actively seek a professional opinion/diagnosis during most of primary school."

Carole, parent of dyslexic

In Carole's case, there was so much interaction and communication that her daughter was well supported and nothing extra was needed. This is fantastic!

Some parents are willing to do research about dyslexia themselves, and some even attend training events. Some are all too happy to support the school with finding solutions and developing strategies for their child (and others). Others struggle themselves with literacy. If a child has dyslexia, there is a statistical chance that the parent does too, whether diagnosed or not. There is still, tragically, a stigma around adult literacy difficulties, and some parents feel ill-equipped to support their child in learning to read.

The key message is to listen. Don't be afraid to reiterate to parents that they can be honest about their own difficulties with you, and with their children. The role of the parent is not to educate, but to support, nurture and enable. Parents need to hear this message. Equally, don't feel undermined by parents who are willing to do research and find strategies themselves. Embrace this useful resource!

Voices of Dyslexia

"I think it's about recognising that we're all very much on an education journey. It's not something that we all immediately know the answers to. I do think it's difficult for teachers in large classes with numerous pupils to support. So I think it's just arming people with the knowledge so that they can feel confident supporting. It's very much a journey and one that we're all in together, parents and teachers working together, trying to seek out the best solutions for the children."

Lisa Barclay, parent[2]

THE IMPORTANCE OF LISTENING

I have known circumstances when collaboration has been less effective, however. Some children repeatedly complain to parents that they can't keep up with the learning, but parents are told by school that they are doing well. These children have learned how to mask their difficulties in school, but at home, it's a different story. Listening to and believing parents can make a huge difference to a child's school experience. I have even known children whose "hidden" dyslexia has been misdiagnosed as behavioural problems or school-based anxiety, and children who have been diagnosed with autism and/or ADHD, but who also have undetected dyslexia. In these cases, parents felt they had not been listened to regarding the dyslexia.

> *"I knew my daughter had some difficulties from early on. She was so easy from birth to three, but then I noticed lots of defiant behaviour, slow to pick up words, struggles with clothing, etc. Then in Reception, she struggled with phonics, reading and writing. She started avoidant behaviours when it came to work: during phonics lessons she would tell the teacher they were wrong constantly and scribble over her work. Behaviour and autism specialists were called in."*
>
> Nicki, parent

In Nicki's daughter's case, concerns about reading and writing, which were significantly impacting on her learning, were ignored for years until she was completely disillusioned with school and educated in alternative provision. I wonder if this could have been avoided.

> *"I just can't wait for my son to leave primary school. I feel so frustrated; I've been labelled as a problem parent throughout and nothing seems to have been done to support him."*
>
> Kerri, parent

SHARE THE GOOD!

Parents of children with special educational needs often hear about what their child is struggling with and how to help. Don't forget, in your limited time, to share the strengths as well. There are always great things to share about children with dyslexia!

THE BALANCE BETWEEN SUPPORTING PARENTS AND MANAGING EXPECTATIONS

When a child has dyslexia, it's really common for parents to be on the receiving end of the associated frustration. Children who are cooperative in class can be the opposite at home, especially when it comes to homework and literacy activities.

"I think advice for parents is just patience and understanding. I know that seems a very obvious thing to say, but it can be very frustrating as a parent when you just want your child to read. And I think in the early stages, before you know that your child has dyslexia or you start to realise there's something else going on, it can be frustrating. And I think it's important that your child's confidence doesn't dip. So just lots of patience, lots of understanding, just being there for your child."

Pippa, parent

Sometimes signposting parents to support groups is invaluable. Sometimes, just offering empathy and a listening ear to these parents is the most valuable and impactful support you can offer.

"There's a parent dyslexia group which I've recently joined, and this has been great to get together with other parents just to find out a bit more tips, hints, things that we're struggling with and where we can support each other."

Lisa Barclay

While some parents would like to be listened to more, some teachers are overwhelmed with demands from parents that they cannot meet, whether because of school budget constraints or because parents are not well informed about what is realistic and necessary for their child. Hopefully, this book has offered manifold ways to support children with dyslexia without needing expensive interventions for every child with dyslexia; communicating these strategies to parents can alleviate anxiety. The best way to manage these expectations is to engage, listen and pre-empt.

QUICK WINS

Here are some easy, prep-free ideas for collaborating with parents that you can do straight away.

Quick Win 1:
In your next newsletter, tell parents about a local dyslexia support group or national dyslexia organisation.

Quick Win 2:
In your next conversation with a parent of a child with literacy difficulties, acknowledge that it must be hard for them.

Quick Win 3:
Ask a parent of a dyslexic child if they would like to contribute to developing some school strategies.

NOTES

1 Pippa's story on film can be found on the Vloices of Dyslexia project page, https://louiseselbydyslexia.com/voices-of-dyslexia-do-you-have-a-story-to-tell
2 Lisa's story can be found on film on the Voices of Dyslexia project page, https://louiseselbydyslexia.com/voices-of-dyslexia-do-you-have-a-story-to-tell

APPENDICES

APPENDIX 1: HOW TO INTERPRET A DIAGNOSTIC REPORT

Reports can be bewildering and overwhelming to the non-specialist. This chapter seeks to explain the function, content and terminology of diagnostic assessment reports.

WHO DIAGNOSES DYSLEXIA?

This can be undertaken by specialist teacher assessors (STAs), who have achieved the Level 7 qualification, or educational psychologists (EPs). Reports will look different according to which type of professional wrote them.

WHAT'S THE DIFFERENCE BETWEEN EP AND STA ASSESSMENTS?

EPs are not required to be trained teachers. Some specialise in dyslexia, while all are qualified and experienced in identifying and diagnosing a range of needs in addition to dyslexia. They are therefore an ideal choice for assessing learners with complex needs. STAs are experienced teachers, and therefore very well placed to offer a range of personalised recommendations for the classroom.

Usually, EPs use formal assessments, but they may also use dynamic assessment techniques which focus more on response and dialogue and do not produce "scores". Some EPs may refer to "specific learning difficulties/differences" rather than more specific terminology such as "dyslexia" or "dyscalculia".

STA reports usually follow a consistent structure in compliance with the SpLD Assessment Standards Committee (SASC), and while the tests can be different, they all cover the same areas. For STA reports to be valid for Disabled Students' Allowance, the assessor must hold an Assessment Practising Certificate, and therefore the report must comply with SASC standards.

WHAT SHOULD I LOOK FOR IN A REPORT?

Assessment reports will bring together a full profile, with scores, alongside observation and qualitative information, with consideration of background information. Reports should include:

1. OVERVIEW

Usually at the beginning, this consists of 2–3 pages. It should include a summary of recommendations, but readers should bear in mind it will not include all the references and resources, which come in the main recommendations section of the report, or appendices.

2. BACKGROUND INFORMATION

Assessors gather information prior to assessment about the learner's early development, education history and current functioning in school and at home. This involves parent, school and child views.

3. COGNITIVE ABILITY

Cognitive skills assessments look at different types of ability. These include:

- **Tests of underlying ability:** These tests are a good indicator of a learner's ability where literacy is not a factor.
    - **Verbal ability:** types of verbal ability are reasoning with words and language, the ability to define, compare or understand vocabulary.

- **Visual ability:** types of visual ability are reasoning, usually involving patterns and shapes, visual-spatial awareness.
- **Crystallised intelligence** refers to abilities which rely on drawing from past experience and knowledge. Some tests of vocabulary, for example, are referred to as crystallised intelligence.
- **Fluid intelligence** refers to ability to reason and think flexibly, without relying on past experience and knowledge. Some visual reasoning tests are referred to as fluid reasoning.

- **Tests of memory**
    - **Working memory:** refers to the ability to hold information in mind and work on it in some way. This can be verbal (usually digits or letters) or visual (pictures, movements or symbols). It can be known as digit, letter or picture span. Working memory also comprises short-term memory and phonological memory.
    - **Short-term memory:** refers to the ability to hold on to and store information for a short period.
    - **Phonological memory:** refers to the ability to process and temporarily store sequences of sounds.
- **Tests of processing speed (verbal and sometimes visual)**
    - **Rapid symbolic naming:** refers to the ability to quickly name aloud a series of items (letters, numbers or pictures) printed on a page.
    - **Coding:** the child works within a specified time limit and uses a key to copy symbols that correspond with simple geometric shapes or numbers.
    - **Symbol search:** the learner scans search groups and indicates whether target symbols are present while working within a specified time limit.
- **Tests of phonological awareness**
    - These tests inform you how well a learner manipulates and discriminates speech sounds. There are a number

of different names for these tests: elision, blending, segmenting, rhyming, spoonerisms are examples. Sometimes a test of phonological awareness using non-words is used.

4. ATTAINMENT

This area involves reading, writing, spelling and sometimes maths. It's useful to compare performance across different tests. Some tests measure speed and efficiency, while some focus on accuracy or comprehension/expression. It's also worth comparing performance of reading or spelling in single words and within texts.

5. DIAGNOSTIC DECISION/CONCLUSIONS

This section should give you not only a diagnostic decision but an explanation of why the decision has been reached and an outline of the individual's learning profile, including strengths and weaknesses. It should give some indicators of cognitive barriers or strengths which inform practice.

6. RECOMMENDATIONS

This is the "so what?" part of the report. Recommendations should be actionable by school and parents, but remember that assessors must meet professional standards and make recommendations depending on a child's needs. Assessors are required to think further ahead as well. Assessors are aware that schools will not be able to implement all the recommendations at one particular time, and parents should also be made aware of this. I love the analogy of recommendations as a menu, which I have borrowed from my colleague, Dr Katharine Sharpe, an EP. It's there to pick and choose, for what works at that time.

WHAT DO THE DIFFERENT TYPES OF SCORES MEAN?

A table of scores, which shows how to compare different types of scores and descriptors, is available for download as online Support Material. Types of scores are described as follows:

STANDARD SCORES

Most commonly used in diagnostic reports, and required for examination access arrangements, a standard score measures the individual's performance against other learners of the same age. Statistically, approximately 68 per cent of scores will fall between SS85 and SS115 and this is commonly known as the "average range". A standard score of 100 marks the midpoint of this average range. An advantage of standard scores is that you can compare them across any tests which also use standard scores. For the purpose of measuring progress, it helps for practitioners and parents to know that standard scores would not be expected to increase if a learner is making expected progress, while a good indicator of accelerated progress is an increased standard score over time.

SCALED SCORES

These work in exactly the same way as standard scores, but they range from 0 to 19, with 10 as the mean, and a score between 7 and 13 is considered to be the average range.

PERCENTILES

These offer a form of "ranking". A percentile score of 40 would indicate that the individual performed better than 39 per cent of others of the same age; 60 per cent would have scored higher. A percentile can be a helpful indicator of the extremity of their specific difficulty or strength in a certain area. However, percentiles should be interpreted with extreme caution. SS85-115 is the same as percentile 16-84; therefore, it is possible to be on the 16th percentile but still within the average range. Like standard scores and scaled scores, percentiles would not be expected to increase if a learner is making expected progress.

COMPOSITE SCORES

This is an overall score which brings together the scores on a number of subtests.

AGE EQUIVALENTS

An age equivalent is the median raw score for a particular age or grade level. Unlike standard scores, scaled scores and percentiles, age-equivalent scores are expected to increase with time if the learner is making expected progress. Age-equivalent scores can therefore be useful for schools to measure progress.

However, this should be undertaken with extreme caution. They are not precise scores and there are many drawbacks of using them:

- They can give the impression that a child is more advanced (or behind) than they actually are.
- They can inflate progress if a child starts at a particularly low level. As abilities develop more quickly with young children, a six-month delay in a young child is likely to reflect a much more concerning picture than a six-month delay in an older child.
- Reading, writing, spelling and maths are taught in different ways and at different ages in different countries; therefore, it is very difficult to be precise about age equivalents.
- Many adult texts are at or below reading age 15.
- A learner can be within the average range but still a year behind according to age-equivalent scores - and this is more concerning for a 6-year-old than a 15-year-old.
- It is entirely possible for a child to have a "reading age" of 8 for word reading accuracy and 11 for reading comprehension; progression is not always linear and uniform.

DESCRIPTORS

For each test score, a descriptor is given. This describes the range of scores in relation to "average" in which the learner's performance sits. The broad average range for standardised tests (85–115) covers 68 per cent of the population, which means that most people taking these tests will fall into this range. A list of descriptors as they correspond to scores is included in the table at the end of this chapter.

SOME GENERAL POINTERS FOR READING AND INTERPRETING REPORTS

1. Remember the assessment itself is a snapshot of a moment in time. Scores and performance can vary and background information plays a very significant part in any diagnostic decision. In addition, assessors are trained to qualitatively analyse scores in relation to test performance and context. For example, a testee may have employed elaborate strategies or put in an unsustainable amount of effort to achieve their scores.
2. Remember, "dyslexia" is a broad term; look for the skills and areas of challenge within this.
3. Look for suggestions of what strategies and approaches might work and how this will translate across the classroom and at home.
4. Don't be afraid to talk to the assessor, discuss findings and recommendations, ask for clarification if needed, and if the report does not reflect what you know of the child, discuss this with them.

APPENDIX 2: FURTHER RESOURCES

I have a website, where you can find many resources for download, as well as the images taken from the case studies in this book and options for further training. I also post trusted resources on my Facebook page, X and LinkedIn.

louise@louiseselbydyslexia.com
https://twitter.com/LouiseSelby21
www.facebook.com/LouiseSelbyDyslexia
www.linkedin.com/in/louise-selby-dyslexia

DYSLEXIA WEBSITES (TRAINING, INFORMATION AND RESOURCES)

www.patoss-dyslexia.org
www.bdadyslexia.org.uk
www.dyslexiascotland.org.uk
www.dyslexiaguild.org.uk
www.dyslexiaida.org

Louise Selby Dyslexia

FIGURE A.1

www.helenarkell.org.uk
www.sasc.org.uk (assessment standards, definitions and advice for assessors)

OTHER USEFUL WEBSITES

www.understood.org
www.nasen.org.uk
https://educationendowmentfoundation.org.uk
www.senresourcesblog.com
www.dekkocomics.com
www.sensiblesenco.org.uk
www.oakabooks.co.uk
www.theschoolpsychologyservice.com/what-works (interventions)

PUBLISHERS OF "HIGH INTEREST LOW LEVEL" BOOKS

www.barringtonstoke.co.uk
www.ransom.co.uk
www.badgerlearning.co.uk/
www.phonicbooks.co.uk
www.pearson.com
www.raintree.co.uk/

BLOGS

www.thedyslexiaclassroom.com/blog
www.kentdyslexia.co.uk/blog
www.alexquigley.co.uk
www.sendmatters.co.uk/blog
www.studyingwithdyslexiablog.co.uk

PODCASTS

Mind the Gap: Making Education Work Across the Globe
The SEND Network
SENDcast
SEND in the experts
Let's Talk Dyslexia (Dyslexia Scotland)

Evidence into Action
The Evidence Based Education Podcast
Thinking Deeply about Primary Education

ASSISTIVE TECHNOLOGY

www.dyslexic.com
www.callscotland.org.uk

MATHS

www.stevechinn.co.uk
www.ronitbird.co.uk (free games)

RESOURCES

www.littlemindsatwork.org (freebies)
www.smartkids.co.uk
www.tts-group.co.uk (lots of voice recorders and other tech)
www.crossboweducation.com (for visual difficulties)
www.autopresseducation.co.uk
www.partnersineducation.co.uk
www.dyslexiaaction.org.uk/shop
www.lidiastanton.com (visual mnemonics for spelling)

PUBLICATIONS

Dyslexia: A Very Short Introduction, Margaret Snowling
The Neurodiverse Classroom: A Teacher's Guide to Individual Learning Needs and How to Meet Them, Victoria Honeybourne
The Inclusive Classroom, Daniel Sobel and Sara Alston
Barrington Stoke School Spelling Dictionary
The Memory and Processing Guide for Neurodiverse Learners, Alison Patrick
Morph Mastery: A Morphological Intervention for Reading, Spelling and Vocabulary, Louise Selby
Dyslexia and Inclusion: Classroom Approaches for Assessment, Teaching and Learning (3rd Edition), Gavin Reid

Towards a consensus on dyslexia: Findings from a Delphi study, Julia Carroll, Caroline Holden, Philip Kirby, Paul Andrew Thompson and Margaret J. Snowling, https://osf.io/preprints/osf/tb8mp

PARENTS

Many of the websites above also offer resources and support for parents. In addition:

DYSLEXIA. Wrestling with an Octopus: 10 Tips to Help Your Child Thrive in Every Aspect of Life Academically, Socially and Physically, Beth Beamish and Sarah Pitts

Parenting Dyslexia podcast

www.dyslexicmum.co.uk/dyslexia-blog

www.nessy.com/en-gb/dyslexia-explained

Wonderfully Wired Brains: An Introduction to the World of Neurodiversity, Louise Gooding

BIBLIOGRAPHY

Aubin, G. (2022). EEF blog: "Five-a-day" to improve SEND outcomes. https://educationendowmentfoundation.org.uk/news/eef-blog-five-a-day-to-improve-send-outcomes

Beamish, B. and Pitts, S. (2020). *DYSLEXIA. Wrestling with an Octopus: 10 Tips to Help Your Child Thrive in Every Aspect of Life Academically, Socially and Physically*. Merits Publishing

Bridgett, E. (2024). How to develop disciplinary literacy in maths.https://researchschool.org.uk/tudor-grange/news/how-to-develop-disciplinary-literacy-in-maths

Carroll, J., Holden, C., Kirby, P., Thompson, P.A. & Snowling, M.J. (2024). Towards a consensus on dyslexia: Findings from a Delphi study. https://osf.io/preprints/osf/tb8mp

Coope, T. (2024). What happened to Evan's writing? https://louiseselbydyslexia.com/what-happened-to-evans-writing

Corbett, P. and Strong, J. (2016). *Jumpstart! Grammar: Games and Activities for ages 6–14* (2nd edition). Abingdon: Routledge.

Corbett, P. (2024). Talk for Writing. www.talk4writing.com

Department for Education (updated 2023). *The Reading Framework*. www.gov.uk/government/publications/the-reading-framework-teaching-the-foundations-of-literacy

Devine, K. (2022). It's a constant battle: Jamie Oliver discusses his "frustrating and resentful" childhood with the learning difficulty in a lengthy post." Mail Online, 17 October. www.dailymail.co.uk/tvshowbiz/article-11324257/Jamie-Oliver-details-struggle-dyslexia-discussing-frustrating-school-days.html

Dictionary.com (2024). Dyslexia. www.dictionary.com/browse/dyslexia

Duke, N.K. and Cartwright, K.B. (2021). The science of reading progresses: Communicating advances beyond the Simple View of Reading. *Reading Research Quarterly*, *56*(S1), S25–S44.

Dyslexia Scotland (2022). Mind mapping. www.dyslexiascotland.org.uk/leaflets

Dyslexia Scotland. (2022) Dyslexia – transition from primary to secondary school. https://dyslexiascotland.org.uk/wp-content/uploads/2022/05/Transition.pdf

Eastap, L. and Gregory, J (2018). *Dyslexia Friendly Schools Good Practice Guide* (2nd edition). British Dyslexia Association

Education Endowment Foundation (2020). Special Education Needs in Mainstream Schools. https://educationendowmentfoundation.org.uk/education-evidence/guidance-reports/send

Education Endowment Foundation (2021). Metacognition and Self-Regulated Learning. https://educationendowmentfoundation.org.uk/education-evidence/guidance-reports/metacognition

Elliott, J. (2020). It's Time to be Scientific about Dyslexia. *Reading Research Quarterly, 55*(51), 561–575.

Evidence into Action (2023). Metacognition [podcast]. https://evidenceintoaction.podbean.com/e/ep-17-metacognition

Fletcher, H. and Caplan, M. (2014). *Anyone Can Spell It.* Helen Arkell Dyslexia Centre.

Gerber, P.J. (2012). The impact of learning disabilities on adulthood: A review of the evidenced-based literature for research and practice in adult education. *Journal of Learning Disabilities, 45*(1), 31–46.

Goodsall, H. and Flohr, S. (2022). *The Dyslexia Handbook 2022.* British Dyslexia Association.

Green, J. (2024). Reading for meaning in science. https://thescienceteacher.co.uk/reading-for-meaning-in-science

Hall, E. (1976). *Beyond Culture.* New York: Knopf Publishing Group.

HM Government (2022). *SEND Review: Right support, right place, right time. Government consultation on the SEND and alternative provision system in England.* https://assets.publishing.service.gov.uk/government/uploads/system/uploads/attachment_data/file/1063620/SEND_review_right_support_right_place_right_time_accessible.pdf

Honeybourne, V. (2018). *The Neurodiverse Classroom: A Teacher's Guide to Individual Learning Needs and How to Meet Them.* London: Jessica Kingsley Publishers.

Hornigold, J. (2024). *All About Dyscalculia: A Practical Guide for Primary Teachers.* Abingdon: Routledge.

Kent Dyslexia (2021). Transition - Primary to Secondary transition tips. https://kentdyslexia.co.uk/blog/f/transition---primary-to-secondary-transition-tips

Kirby, P. and Snowling, M. (2022). *Dyslexia, a History*. Montreal: McGill-Queens University Press.

Lavan, G. and Talcott, J.B. (2020). *What Works for Literacy Difficulties?* (6th edition). www.theschoolpsychologyservice.com/what-works

Macdonald, S. (2019). From "disordered" to "diverse": Defining six sociological frameworks employed in the study of dyslexia in the UK. *Insights on Learning Disabilities*, *16*(1), 1-22.

Miller, J. (2024). 6 surprising ways dyslexia affects math and how to help. Made for Math. https://madeformath.com/dyslexia-affects-math

Morgan, W.P. (1896). A Case of Congenital Word Blindness. *British Medical* Journal, *2*(1871), 1378.

Moseley, S. (2023). *Teaching Reading to All Learners Including Those with Complex Needs*. Abingdon: Routledge.

Muter, V. (2021). *Understanding and Supporting Children with Literacy Difficulties*. Jessica Kingsley Publishers.

Newton, F. (2023). *Inclusive PE for SEND Children: A Practical Guide for Teachers*. FB3 Publishing

Newton, F. (2024). Inclusive PE strategies cheat sheet. School OT. www.schoolot.co.uk/resources

Orton-Gillingham Academy (n.d.). What is the Orton-Gillingham approach? www.ortonacademy.org/resources/what-is-the-orton-gillingham-approach

Packer, N. (2019). Supporting dyslexia in the maths classroom. Maths No Problem! https://mathsnoproblem.com/blog/learner-focus/supporting-dyslexia-maths-classroom

PANS/PANDAS UK (n.d.). What are PANS and PANDAS? www.panspandasuk.org/what-are-pans-and-pandas

Patrick, A. (2020). *The Memory and Processing Guide for Neurodiverse Learners*. Jessica Kingsley Publishers.

Potter, C. and Rowland, M. (2024). Pupil premium and SEND: learning without labels. Unity Research School, https://researchschool.org.uk/unity/news/pupil-premium-and-send-learning-without-labels

Quigley, A. (2018). *Closing the Vocabulary Gap*. Abingdon: Routledge.

Quigley, A. (2020). *Closing the Reading Gap*. Abingdon: Routledge.

Quigley, A. (2022). *Closing the Writing Gap*. Abingdon: Routledge.

Quigley, A. (2023) Why might Chat GPT damage learning? https://alexquigley.co.uk/why-might-chatgpt-damage-learning

Reid, G. (2018). 20 teaching ideas and strategies to support students with dyslexia. www.teachit.co.uk/cpd/send/20-teaching-ideas-support-dyslexia

Reid, G. (2020). *Dyslexia and Inclusion: Classroom Approaches for Assessment, Teaching and Learning*. Abingdon: Routledge.

Rooke, M. (2017). *Dyslexia is My Superpower (Most of the Time)*. London: Jessica Kingsley Publishers.

Rose, J. (2009). Identifying and Teaching Children and Young People with Dyslexia and Literacy Difficulties: An independent report from Sir Jim Rose to the Secretary of State for Children, Schools and Families, June 2009. www.thedyslexia-spldtrust.org.uk/media/downloads/inline/the-rose-report.1294933674.pdf

Ross, H. (2024). *KS3–4. Dyslexia: Supporting Neurodiversity*. www.teachit.co.uk/resources/all-subjects/dyslexia-toolkit

Selby, L. (2021). *Morph Mastery: A Morphological Intervention for Reading, Spelling and Vocabulary*. Abingdon: Speechmark.

Snowling, M. (2024). Dyslexia and Language – Disorder or Difference? Lecture at Gresham College. YouTube. www.youtube.com/watch?v=j_dSQQwpoR8

Snowling, M. (2017). Dyslexia. Tes Podagogy podcast.

Snowling, M.J. (2019). *Dyslexia: A Very Short Introduction*. Oxford: Oxford University Press.

Sobel, D. and Alston, S, (2021). *The Inclusive Classroom*. London: Bloomsbury Education.

Specialist Teacher Assessor Standards Committee (2022). SASC – Format for a Pre-16 Diagnostic Assessment Report for Specific Learning Difficulties. https://sasc.org.uk/media/cbfdeheu/pre-16-years-assessment-report-format-sasc-may-2022.pdf

Stanton, L. (2016). *200 Tricky Spellings in Cartoons*. Lidia Stanton.

Stanton, L. (2017). *Tricky Spellings in Cartoons for Children, Part 1*. Lidia Stanton.

Stone, L. (2021). *Spelling for Life*. Abingdon: Routledge.

Suresh, S. (2021). Does school culture eat strategy for breakfast? Teach First. www.teachfirst.org.uk/blog/school-culture-strategy

UK House of Lords Judgment (Phelps), https://publications.parliament.uk/pa/ld199900/ldjudgmt/jd000727/phelp-1.htm

University of Oxford (n.d.). The UK Dyslexia Archive. https://dyslexiahistory.web.ox.ac.uk/uk-dyslexia-archive

Wade, J. (n.d.) Sounds and Syllables. https://jwed.co.uk/spelling

WEBSITES

British Dyslexia Association – www.bdadyslexia.org.uk

Call Scotland – www.callscotland.org.uk

Dekko Comics – www.dekkocomics.com

Dyslexia Scotland – www.dyslexiascotland.org.uk

Dyslexic.com – www.dyslexic.com

Education Endowment Foundation – www.educationendowmentfoundation.org.uk

Helen Arkell Dyslexia Charity – www.helenarkell.org.uk

Joint Council for Qualifications – www.jcq.org.uk/

International Dyslexia Association – www.dyslexiaida.org

Musescore, https://musescore.org/en

Pocket Study Skills series – www.bloomsbury.com/uk/series/pocket-study-skills

Professional Association of Teachers of Students with Specific Learning Difficulties (PATOSS) – www.patoss-dyslexia.org

SpLD Assessment Standards Committee – www.sasc.org.uk

Understood – www.understood.org

INDEX